SHADOW & SUBSTANCE

AFRO-AMERICAN EXPERIENCE IN CONTEMPORARY CHILDREN'S FICTION

RUDINE SIMS

Abigail E. Weeks
Memorial Library
Union College

presented by

Shadow and Substance

Dedicated with love and gratitude to the memory of Mom and Dad—Lucille M. (Hodge) Sims and Beark Myer Sims. They kept their hands on the plow and held on, believing that somehow education—and books—would one day make me free.

Shadow and Substance

Afro-American Experience in
Contemporary Children's Fiction

Rudine Sims
University of Massachusetts

National Council of Teachers of English
1111 Kenyon Road, Urbana, Illinois 61801

NCTE Stock Number 43768

Library of Congress Cataloging in Publication Data

Sims, Rudine, 1937–
    Shadow and substance.

    Bibliography: p.
    1. Children's stories—History and criticism.
2. Afro-Americans in literature. I. Title.
PS374.C45S55   813'.54'093520396073   82-6518
ISBN 0-8141-4376-8   AACR2

Contents

Beware lest you lose the substance by grasping at the shadow.

Aesop

Preface

As recently as 1965, Black children exploring the world of children's books found themselves looking into a kind of distorted fun-house mirror that resisted sending back reflections at all, or sent out only laughable or unrecognizable images. Fortunately, that situation has changed. This monograph presents an analysis of the nature and extent of that change.

The purpose of the monograph is to provide classroom teachers, librarians, and teacher-educators in the field of children's literature with information that will enable them to make better informed selections of literature for and about Afro-Americans. Purists suggest that literature is its own excuse for being, and that to judge children's books on criteria other than literary ones is to debase literature and to burden its creators with a responsibility not really theirs. Purists notwithstanding, educators who choose books for children cannot separate literary evaluations from social responsibility. The literature we choose helps to socialize our children and to transmit to them our values. My hope is that the information provided here may lead readers to a greater awareness of the range of values and attitudes to be found in modern children's fiction about Afro-Americans.

This monograph reports on a survey and analysis of 150 books of contemporary realistic fiction about Afro-Americans published from 1965 to 1979 inclusive. These books are appropriate for young people from preschool through eighth grade. The sample is not random, leaning heavily on the New York Public Library's comprehensive annotated bibliography, *The Black Experience in Children's Books* (Rollock, 1974, 1979), and on the James Weldon Johnson Memorial Collection at the Countee Cullen Branch of that library, where the books listed in the bibliography are housed. The sample, however, is representative of the types of fiction about Blacks produced during the period in question.

In order to emphasize images of today's children, books of historical fiction, particularly of the painful slavery era, have been deliberately excluded. While the fiction in the survey is referred to as contemporary in setting, in the case of children's literature it is sometimes difficult to know how far back in time one can go before material ceases to be contemporary for a child, especially a young one. For the most part, the books in this survey are set in the latter part of the twentieth century. A few picture books are set in an earlier time but are contemporary in feeling, with their historical setting making no difference to the story, though it may influence the style of the art.

The terms *Afro-American* and *Black* are used throughout. Afro-American, a subcategory of Black, was deliberately chosen to emphasize that the books in the survey are limited to those about growing up Black in the United States, as distinct from Africa, the Caribbean, or Central or South America. The term *Black*, capitalized as the label for a distinct cultural group, is used in a more generic sense.

Acknowledgments

Special thanks are owed and hereby offered to the following people who helped to make this book possible:

To the staff of the Countee Cullen Branch of the New York Public Library, especially Mrs. Vivian Delaney, for the gracious manner in which they made the James Weldon Johnson Collection easily accessible, arranged extended working time for me, and made the working environment extremely comfortable and pleasant.

To the Allens—Hattie, Oscar, Carol, and Adele—for generously making their home mine during my stay in New York; and to Dr. Curtis Lawson, who joined his sister's family in treating me like visiting royalty during my stay.

To Professor Byrd L. Jones, friend and colleague at the University of Massachusetts, for reading the draft of the manuscript and providing me with both encouragement and insightful and supportive criticisms.

To Professor Charles A. Frye, of Hampshire College, good friend and superb listener, for acting as a very patient and very effective sounding board, and for his generous sharing of information and insights about Afro-American culture and experience.

1 The Context for Change

I've been 'buked, and I've been scorned.
I've been talked about, sho's you born!

Traditional Spiritual

There is power in The Word. People in positions of power over others have historically understood, and often feared, the potential of The Word to influence the minds of the people over whom they hold sway. This fear manifests itself in both dramatic and mundane ways—from the burning of books to organized book bannings to parents' censoring of their own children's reading. Strong evidence of this fear and respect can be found in the history of Euro-American slavery: the forced separation of Africans from others who spoke the same language, laws forbidding teaching Afro-American slaves to read, and the eagerness of many Afro-Americans to risk their own safety in learning to read and in teaching others. In the world of Afro-Americans, this respect for The Word was evident, too, in the early development of a formal Afro-American literature, beginning even before the United States became an independent nation. And it was partly through folk literature and lore that early Afro-Americans were able to gain a sense of control over their own lives and the strength to survive in an alien land.

Literature, which is the artistic, culturally valued form of The Word, serves an important function in society. The noted Black author James Baldwin (Watkins, 1979) expresses it this way: "Literature is indispensable to the world. . . . The world changes according to the way people see it, and if you alter, even by a millimeter, the way a person looks at reality, then you can change it." This belief in the power of literature to change the world underlies most of the controversies in the field of children's literature. In particular, it underlies current concerns about contemporary realistic fiction—its topics, its themes, its inclusion of nontraditional values and life-styles. Many parents, teachers, and librarians, seeing children as susceptible to the influence of books, fear that today's literature will help to acquaint their children with worlds they themselves never knew and with which they are unprepared to cope. Others, such as women, Blacks, and other so-called minorities, fear that literature will reinforce and perpetuate the racism and sexism that have had such negative effects on their lives and on society in general. Research evidence is mixed, but in reviewing the literature, Chall, Radwin, French, and Hall (1979) found studies to support the contention that children's books do have the power to affect self-concept and world view. Concern about the potential of children's literature to influence readers' attitudes about themselves and others and to increase social awareness is at the crux of arguments about the image of Blacks in children's fiction and about the authenticity of Afro-American experience as mirrored in those books.

Historically, the Afro-American child in the world of children's books had indeed been, in the words of the spiritual, " 'buked and scorned." Less than two decades ago, Larrick (1965) notified the American public through *Saturday Review* that the world of children's books was, in her terms, "all-white." She had discovered that of the 5,206 children's books published in 1962, 1963, and 1964, only 6.7 percent (349) included even one Black child in either text or illustrations. She asserted that this situation was harmful to Black and white children alike.

The Larrick revelation was timely, coming at a period when many people believed that the United States was facing a racial crisis, and when the Civil Rights Movement was becoming the Black Revolution. Larrick's article was published a year before Stokely Carmichael popularized the Black Power slogan, and eleven years after the United States Supreme Court had declared "separate but equal" schools to be inherently unequal.

The previous decade had been a roller coaster of hope and despair. In 1955, Rosa Parks's refusal to give up her seat on a bus had triggered the Montgomery bus boycott and the rise to prominence of Martin Luther King, Jr. In 1957, President Dwight Eisenhower had to call in the National Guard to help desegregate Little Rock's Central High School. The lunch counter sit-ins began in Greensboro, North Carolina, in 1960. The year 1963 was one of turmoil: Bull Connor used dogs and water hoses on marchers in Birmingham, Alabama; Medgar Evers, of the Mississippi NAACP, was murdered; Governor George Wallace "stood in the schoolhouse door" to prevent the desegregation of the University of Alabama; four Black girls attending Sunday School were killed by a bomb thrown into their Birmingham church; and President John F. Kennedy was assassinated. In the midst of those despairing events, the March on Washington for Jobs and Freedom, on August 28, 1963, drew 200,000 people in an optimistic effort to make Americans, and especially Congress, aware that 100 years after Emancipation, Afro-Americans were still not free. The following year, 1964, Congress passed the Civil Rights Act, but the turmoil continued; three civil rights workers were murdered in Mississippi. In 1965, the year the Larrick article was published, Malcolm X was murdered in February; and in August, Watts, the Black section of Los Angeles, exploded in flames.[1]

These events were widely publicized, making the American public aware that all was not well with the souls of Black folk in the United States. It was also in 1965 that Congress passed the Elementary and Secondary Education Act, which made available some $1.3 billion to the nation's schools. The time, then, was ripe for publishers to respond to Larrick's challenge by producing more books about Black children. Liberal consciences had been deeply pricked by the events of the previous decade, and federal money made it possible for school districts and libraries to spend large sums on books. Thus, a market was created for books about Black children.

Fourteen years after the publication of the Larrick report, Chall et al. (1979) conducted a similar study in an effort to gauge progress. They surveyed 4,775 children's trade books published in 1973, 1974, and 1975, eleven years after the publication of the books in the Larrick study. Their survey found that the percentages of books including at least one Black in the text or illustrations had more than doubled to 14.4 percent (689). It might appear that this doubling of quantity was sufficient to permit a self-congratulatory complacence among the publishers of children's books. However, for the 14.4 percent of children's books that did include Blacks, there were 85.6 percent that did not. A large percentage of those non-Black books were likely to be all-white; that is, they were not likely to include any other nonwhite people, either.

Moreover, the issue of the near invisibility of the Black child was compounded by the issue of negative images. The Black child historically had not only been " 'buked and scorned," but "talked

---

1. This brief overview is taken for the most part from J. H. Franklin, *From Slavery to Freedom*, 3d ed. (New York: Alfred A. Knopf, 1967).

about" as well. To be "talked about," in the sense of the spiritual, is no better than being ignored, since it suggests malicious gossip, undeserved notoriety. It suggests again the power of The Word to create images.

In a discussion of images, critic Carolyn Gerald (1972) asserted that an author as image-maker can shape a reader's reality by using artistic language to provoke an emotional response and to "dim out of our consciousness" all other possible alternative points of view. The image-maker, for example, can make us see a rose bush as pleasant because of its scent, or dangerous because of its thorns, or as a metaphor for pleasure gained only at the expense of pain, depending on the author's own perspective, intent, and skills. For people who have been nearly invisible or made the object of ridicule, the image-maker has the vast potential for changing their world by changing both the way they see themselves and the way they are seen by others.

Gerald's statement on the importance of image to Afro-Americans is a compelling argument, not only for increasing their visibility, but for authentic cultural images:

> ... man projects his cultural and racial images upon the universe and he derives a sense of personal worth from the reflection he sees gazing back at him. For he defines himself and the world in terms of others like him. He discovers his identity within a group.
>
> And now we come to the heart of the matter, for we cannot judge ourselves unless we see a continuity in other people and in things and concepts. We question our very right to exist without other existences like our own. This is why image is so important to Afro-Americans. We are a black people living in a white world. [P. 373]

Gerald then went on to point out that much of the time Black people in this country see either no image of themselves, or a negative one—"subservient to, or uncomfortably different from, or busy emulating the larger, all-inclusive white culture" (p. 373). This condition is reflected in the world of children's books.

That the image of Blacks in children's books has historically been a negative one has been well documented by Broderick (1973) in her analysis of the portrayal of Blacks in children's fiction from 1827 to 1967. She presented numerous examples of the negative and demeaning images of Blacks that had been perpetrated up to that time, making it clear that even when Blacks did appear in children's books, they were there primarily to be "talked about."

By the late sixties and early seventies, when publishers had had time to respond to the Larrick challenge and market opportunities,

These are "melting pot" books in which, in most cases, only the illustrations give any indication that the book is about Black children. Sometimes these books are actually about white children. Quite frequently they place Black children in racially integrated settings. Often they are described as telling "universal" stories, with which Any Child (read "white middle-class child") can identify.

Thirty years after Wright's *Blueprint for Negro Writers*, Killens (1971) issued another challenge:

> Along with the fight to desegregate the schools, we must desegregate the entire cultural statement of America; we must desegregate the minds of the American people. If we merely succeed in desegregating the school buildings, we may very well find that we have won the battle and lost the war. Integration begins the day after the minds of the American people are desegregated. This is the great challenge to all American writers, but especially to the black writer. Who will tell the real story of America if the black writer doesn't? [P. 388]

Killens assumed a white audience and a Black one as well. His was a demand that history, both factual history and history in a literary sense, be rewritten truthfully; that Black writers tell their stories from a Black frame of reference; that white writers explore, for example, the effects of racism and oppression on white people. The Killens argument, in terms of children's literature, is for an increase in the quantity of Black writers and for a receptive audience of Blacks and whites.

Killens was writing at a time when many young Black writers (for example, Leroi Jones/Imamu Baraka, Ron Karenga) were advocating a revolutionary Black nationalist literature, addressed to Blacks, that rejected white American/West European cultural values and aesthetics and that reflected solely Black culture, aesthetics, and consciousness. Their demands were not unlike the call for a break with European literary traditions and the development of an American nationalist literature issued in the nineteenth century by people like Emerson, Trumbull, and Noah Webster. In children's fiction about Blacks, the effect of the Black nationalist literary movement was seen in the assumption of an audience of Black readers, which influenced Black writers to focus on settings, themes, styles, and even forms that were not found in the social conscience books or the melting pot books—for example, the meaning of "soul," the strengths that enabled Black families to survive, various forms of Black English, and the idea, in the words of Nikki Giovanni's poem "Nikki Rosa," that "Black love is Black wealth."

Considerations of the audience to whom books about Afro-Americans are primarily addressed cannot be dissociated from other factors that influence the quality of such books. The issue cannot be simplified to suggest that the audience for books about Blacks is, in any case, either all-Black or all-white. As Lester pointed out in the letter to Woods mentioned previously, a book written by Blacks for Blacks is not closed to whites. The point is that there is a difference between being talked *to* and being talked *about*, between being subject and being audience, and that such a difference manifested itself in books about Afro-American children.

How Is the Term *Afro-American Experience* to Be Interpreted?

Issues of audience are obviously related to issues of content and theme. Many teachers and librarians think books about Afro-American experience are meant for Black children only. In their minds, the Afro-American experience is equated with the hardships and social problems they associate with growing up Black and poor in the city—fatherless homes, gangs, drugs, tough or obscene language, police brutality, crime, and so forth. Therefore, they reason, "Black experience" books are so far removed from the experiences of white children as to be irrelevant at best, or too harsh and inexplicable at worst. In the minds of these same people, stories in which such hardships play no role and children face no racially motivated conflicts are not "Black experience" stories at all. Like the blinded Philip in Theodore Taylor's *The Cay* (New York: Doubleday, 1969), who finally recognizes Timothy's humanness but has to ask whether Timothy is still Black, many teachers and librarians are unable to recognize that "Black experience" is also "human experience."

Narrow and limiting definitions of what constitutes Black experience are neither unique to teachers nor without historical precedent. The talented Black writer Walter Dean Myers (1979) related in an article in the *Interracial Books for Children Bulletin* that some editors have tried to place limits on his writing by their unwillingness to accept, for example, the presence of a white child in a Black neighborhood, or language that did not fit their definitions of Black dialect. Historically, it is well known that the careers of many Black artists, such as Paul Laurence Dunbar and Zora Neale Hurston, were often constrained by the attitudes and resulting actions of their white patrons and the buying public, who were willing to accept only those images of Blacks that matched their own.[2] When narrowly circumscribed definitions of Afro-American experience are held by publishers and editors, they can limit opportunities for Black authors to make unique contributions. Such definitions also belie the variety and complexity to be found in Afro-American experience.

Underlying these narrow views of what constitutes Afro-American experience is an assumption that Black culture, as reflected in such books, is a monolithic "culture of poverty," and that Afro-Americans are otherwise simply like other Americans except for darker skins. Robert Blauner (1970) argued that misconceptions about Black culture arose from a misapplication of the traditional model of immigrant ethnic group assimilation. Because Africans brought to this country were denied just those elements that would have identified them as an ethnic group (a common language, an identification with a national homeland), some sociologists asserted that no distinctive culture remained to Afro-Americans. However, Blauner argued that the very elimination of those traditional elements created the right conditions for the development of a distinctive culture that was *Afro-American* in nature. He asserted that it is both an ethnic and a class culture (not a culture of poverty) because the Afro-American experience produced a "residue of shared collective memories and frames of reference" (p. 352). Blauner further cited what he said were some of the sources of these "collective memories": Africa, slavery, the South, Emancipation, northern migration, and, above all, racism. Racism, he said, has consolidated, rather than eliminated, the distinctive experiences of the past.

Levine (1977) characterized culture as a process, ultimately the result of the interaction of the past and the present. Afro-American culture, he suggested, is the result of transformations, interactions between an African world view and a Euro-American world view, which created a new and distinct Afro-American perspective. Thus, one who grows up Black in this country develops a sensibility, a frame of reference, a perspective on the world that is peculiarly Afro-American.

---

2. See the discussion of Hurston's relationship with her wealthy patron in R. Hemenway, *Zora Neale Hurston: A Literary Biography* (Urbana: University of Illinois Press, 1977), especially pp. 104–58 *passim.* See also Z. Hurston, "What White Publishers Won't Print," *Negro Digest* 8 (April 1950): 85–90; and chapter six, "Black Creativity and American Attitudes," in H. Baker, *The Journey Back: Issues in Black Literature and Criticism* (Chicago: University of Chicago Press, 1980), especially p. 152, for a discussion of Dunbar and William Dean Howells.

This distinct perspective, however, is shared by Afro-Americans across a wide range of individual experiences and social and economic circumstances. From the early history of Afro-Americans, the experiences of individuals, groups, and families have varied. Even during the height of nineteenth-century slavery, there were Blacks whose material circumstances permitted them to live better than low-income whites and much like middle- or upper-income whites. In today's world, Afro-Americans continue to reflect a wide range of experiences and circumstances. However, the experience of growing up as the child of an Afro-American physician, or lawyer, or college professor is as valid—and as Afro-American— as that of growing up the child of a Black cleaning woman, or in a household dependent on welfare. All Blacks are touched by or participate in what Blauner called shared collective memories and frames of reference.

The fact that Afro-Americans are simultaneously a part of the more general American culture and a distinct cultural group is reflected in Afro-American literature as well as in the rest of Afro-American life. Baker (1980) affirmed that Afro-American texts, from their published beginnings with Phillis Wheatley's poetry, have preserved and communicated "culturally unique meanings." Part of this cultural uniqueness has been what Baker called a "functional opposition"; that is, the urge toward the larger society has been in opposition to the writer's attempts to produce works that appeal to a "Black cultural collectivity."

As it relates to children's literature, Hamilton discussed the issue of cultural uniqueness in terms of an Afro-American sensibility. In an article entitled "High John Is Risen Again" (1975a), she asserted that a nonwhite literature is essential and is itself "a vanguard, a continuing revelation of a people's essence and individuality" (p. 117). Her challenge to today's Black writers was to "reach far back and to know again and to trust the sensibilities of slave ancestors" (p. 114). She continued:

> Just as slave art created High John de Conqueror and all manner of other beings out of oppression, so must non-white literature project its own ethos from today's subtle encounter. Our present experience is not one and the same with the oppression of slave times. While we are not totally free, neither are we totally captured. For never before has black creative intelligence coincided so opportunely with the development of black pride, the advancement of political-cultural awareness, independence, and style to affect black art. Not in our Renaissance of the 1920's was so broad a base of black people ever so involved in self- and group-assertion. [P. 116]

In that same article, Hamilton declared that she "attempts to recognize the unquenchable spirit that I know exists in my race and in other races, in order to rediscover a universality within myself" (p. 120). The recognition of universality within the particulars of a distinct cultural experience seems to be lacking in the thinking of those who see "the Black experience" as constricting to a writer. Huck (1979) stated that "there are more Blacks writing and illustrating than ever before. Some of these artists and illustrators are not going to want to be limited to writing about the Black experience. Nor should they be limited in this way" (p. 398). The real limitation is in the failure to recognize that the experience of any distinct cultural group, including Afro-Americans, is broad enough on which to build a body of literature, distinct enough to provide unique perspectives on the world, and universal enough to be worth the effort.

It should be obvious that specifying the contents of Black culture or Afro-American experience would be inherently difficult and is, in any case, beyond the scope of this discussion. The main point here is to reaffirm the reality of the concept and to assert that among those responsible for publishing, buying, and recommending children's books about Afro-Americans, the understanding of the concept needs to be deepened and widened. The other point is that to the extent that the experience of growing up Afro-American is unique, it is reasonable to expect that those who create fiction reflecting that experience have, at the least, some awareness of the perspective from which they are supposedly writing.

What Cultural Perspectives Inform Books about Afro-Americans?

At the other end of the spectrum from those with limited concepts of Afro-American experience are those willing to label any book with an important Black character as a "Black experience" book, and to assume that any author who writes such a book is Black. (Every year some teacher in one of my classes is amazed to discover that Ezra Jack Keats is not an Afro-American.) They are often surprised and disconcerted to learn of controversies over the authenticity of Black experience reflected in children's books about Afro-Americans. At the heart of the controversies about authenticity and, ultimately, the issue of who should be writing books about Afro-American experience lie notions about cultural imperialism versus self-affirmation, and the very idea of the existence of Afro-American literature, particularly in children's books.

Huck (1979), whose textbook on children's literature is widely used, defined the issue in terms of the "racial background of the author. . . . Must an author be black to write about blacks . . .?" (p. 398). To frame the issue in those terms is an oversimplification. It should be clear at this point that not all books about Afro-Americans can be called, or are even intended to be, Afro-American literature. (Some, of course, cannot be called literature in any sense.) That an Afro-American literature exists is undeniable, and the authors of works in that literary tradition are, by definition, Afro-American. If that tradition extends to children's literature, as Virginia Hamilton implied, then, by definition, its authors will be Afro-American, too.

On the other hand, there have been and are Afro-American writers, such as Frank Yerby, who choose not to write Afro-American literature. The issue, then, revolves partly around the intent of the author. Obviously, white authors have been successful, both in a commercial and in a literary sense, in creating fictional stories about Afro-American children. But the best of these have generally been the "melting pot" books, deliberately ignoring any racial or cultural characteristics except skin color and reflecting only the "American" (read "middle-class") side of the Afro-American experience.

The issue also revolves partly around the intended reader. If Broderick's observation is accurate, that what gets into books including Blacks is "what the white adult establishment wants white children to know," then it is not surprising that most authors of children's fiction about Blacks are not Black. (The 150 books in this survey were written by 104 different authors, only 34 of whom are Black.) If, on the other hand, the real need is books that "tell black people about themselves," as Julius Lester indicated, then it is also not surprising that Blacks have demanded that the situation be changed.

The most telling criticism of white authors writing fiction about Afro-American experience has been that their own experiences growing up white in a society that confers automatic and inherent social superiority to that condition have determined the perspective from which they write. Perspective, according to Richard Wright (1972), is "that fixed point in intellectual space where a writer stands to view the struggles, hopes, and suffering of his people" (p. 341). An author arrives at this point by way of personal life experiences, and the argument has been made that the life experiences of Afro-Americans produce a world view that is simultaneously different from and the same as that of other

Americans, but that is not likely to be shared by many white authors.

Hamilton (1978), in an article entitled "Writing the Source: In Other Words," described the source as being what a writer has "dared to live" (p. 619). She wrote about Black people, she stated, because being Black herself, she knew Black people better than any other people:

> The writer uses the most comfortable milieu in which to tell a story, which is why my characters are Black. Often being Black is significant to the story; other times it is not. The writer will always attempt to tell stories no one else can tell. [P. 618]

Assuming that Hamilton is correct, that writers use "the most comfortable milieu," her comments raise an important question. When a white writer tells a fictional "growing up" story from the point of view of a Black child at the center of an Afro-American family (for example, Bette Greene's *Philip Hall Likes Me, I Reckon, Maybe*, 1974, or Louise Fitzhugh's *Nobody's Family Is Going to Change*, 1974), how is that likely to be a story that no one else can tell, a story that is derived from what the writer has "dared to live"? It should not be unexpected that the overall quality of such a work, no matter how skilled a storyteller the writer is, will be diminished because the "fixed point in intellectual space" from which the author views these personal creations remains too far from, and perhaps even in contrast to, the point where an Afro-American would stand to view the struggles and hopes of Black children and their families. The exact location of the point on which those authors stand can only be inferred, but often the specific details used by white authors to convince us of the truth of their vision of Afro-American life are not quite on the mark and suggest an outsider's perspective.

At issue is not simply "racial background," but cultural affinity, sensitivity, and sensibility. Ironically, one of the possible sources from which a writer could gain some understanding of an Afro-American world view or culture or sensibility is through Afro-American literature itself, including folk literature and lore. An Afro-American literature has been extant for more than 200 years, and an oral folk tradition even longer. If Black writers of children's books are provided an opportunity to develop their talents and to continue this literary tradition, they can illuminate for Black and white readers both the uniqueness and the universality of the experience of growing up Afro-American. The irony is that as long as people in positions of relative power in the world of

children's literature—publishers, librarians, educators—insist that
the background of the author does not matter, the opportunities
for Black writers will remain limited, since they will have to com-
pete with established non-Black writers whose perspective on the
Afro-American experience may be more consistent with that of
the editors and publishers and whose opportunities to develop
their talents as writers have been greater.

Summary and Overview

Since 1965 there has been an increase in the quantity of children's
books about Afro-Americans. Given the social forces that seeded
this crop of books, one can assume that the authors of these books,
perhaps to an even greater extent than most writers, set about to
change the world by changing the way children see Black people in
their world.

Authors of contemporary children's fiction about Afro-Americans are greatly influenced by their own view of the world of Afro-
Americans. Authors who accept the concept of an Afro-American
world view and who attempt to convey this world view in their
fiction produce a literature that is distinctive from that written by
those authors who relate a white world view. A second influence
on literature about Afro-Americans is the intended audience. Fiction by Afro-Americans for Afro-American children is clearly
distinguishable from fiction by non-Afro-Americans for non-Afro-
American children. Falling between these two categories of literature is the fiction written by both Afro-Americans and non-Afro-
Americans in which the distinctive Afro-American qualities of
the characters are ignored in the text. Only by looking at the illustrations can the reader determine whether there are Afro-American
characters in the story.

This first chapter has placed contemporary realistic fiction
about Afro-Americans in a sociocultural and historical context.
The chapters that follow examine a substantial portion of the
realistic fiction about Afro-Americans for young people, preschool
through grade eight, published from 1965 to 1979.

Chapter two discusses the "social conscience" books, which are
mainly those characterized by George Woods as being about Blacks
and written to help whites know the condition of their fellow
humans.

Chapter three discusses the "melting pot" books, which probably were written for both Black and white readers on the assump-

tion that both need to be informed that nonwhite children are exactly like other American children, except for the color of their skins.

Chapter four discusses the "culturally conscious" books, which were written primarily, though not exclusively, for Afro-American readers. These books attempt to reflect and illuminate both the uniqueness and the universal humanness of the Afro-American experience from the perspective of an Afro-American child or family.

Chapter five presents brief overviews of the work of five Afro-American writers who have made major contributions to Afro-American children's fiction since 1965.

The final chapter summarizes the current status of children's fiction about Afro-Americans and suggests some frontiers yet to be explored.

2 Realistic Fiction with a Social Conscience

He may mean good, but he do so doggone poor!

Traditional Afro-American Saying

Children's literature, like adult literature, often reflects the social concerns current at the time of its creation. This is no less true of fiction about Afro-American children published since 1965. The very increase in quantity of such books was, in part, a reflection of the belief prevalent in the fifties and early sixties that racial integration would be the prescription that would cure the nation's social ills. "Black and white together," we sang, "we shall overcome."

This faith in the healing power of integration, which was to be preceded by desegregation, was reflected in the content as well as the quantity of children's fiction. This chapter analyzes books focusing on conflicts that develop between Blacks and whites, usually when Blacks move into formerly all-white schools or communities. In this survey, those books are labeled *social conscience* books because they seem clearly intended to create a social conscience—mainly in non-Afro-American readers, to encourage them to develop empathy, sympathy, and tolerance for Afro-American children and their problems. A few, however, almost seem to be "backlash" books, intended to develop Afro-American social consciences by suggesting that the empathy and sympathy must flow two ways; white children have problems, too.

The social conscience books reviewed here, twenty-one in number, comprise the smallest of the three categories of books in this survey. Probably, the 1965 starting date of the survey marks the beginning of the end of an era. The number of social conscience books would be significantly larger if the survey included earlier books. The social conscience books are descendants, for example, of such pioneering books of the 1940s as Jesse Jackson's *Call Me Charley* (New York: Harper and Row, 1945) and Marguerite DeAngeli's *Bright April* (New York: Doubleday, 1946), both of which explored racial prejudice and discrimination. Two other earlier books that also might have been included are Dorothy Sterling's *Mary Jane* (New York: Doubleday, 1959) and Hila Colman's *Classmates by Request* (New York: William Morrow, 1964). As it is, however, three-fourths of the social conscience books in this survey were published between 1965 and 1970, a reflection of changing times and changing attitudes. By 1970, Martin Luther King's dreams of togetherness for the grandchildren of former slaves and the grandchildren of former slaveholders had been shattered on a Memphis motel balcony; and riotous explosions in Los Angeles, Detroit, and other large cities had made it clear that integration had not yet become the miracle cure for the sickness of racism. In addition, by 1970 more works by Afro-American writers were being produced and published, assuring a focus on different themes and topics. By the early seventies, too, criticisms of the social conscience books had begun to reach the eyes and ears of the publishers and authors.

In general, the criticisms suggest that in most cases the social conscience books were created from an ethnocentric, non-Afro-American perspective, which resulted in the perpetuation of undesirable attitudes. The sociological criticisms are bolstered by the fact that these books, as a group, also suffer from literary mediocrity. Many of the plots are highly predictable; many contain implausible, illogical, or contrived episodes. In addition to minor stock characters and stereotypes, many of the major characters are undeveloped clichés. Some of the books are also saddled with pedestrian or downright wretched writing.

A major assumption underlying this study has been that the best books for or about Afro-American children must be both well written and sensitive to cultural and social realities. Such realities dictate that the experience of growing up Afro-American is not the same as growing up white with a brown mask. With literary quality a clear criterion, what follows is an analysis of the social conscience books, guided and informed by a consideration of the three background issues discussed in the first chapter: the inferred primary readership, the awareness of and sensitivity to a uniquely Afro-American life experience, and the perspective from which the books appear to be written.

The Social Conscience Stories

Basically, the social conscience books comprise variations on four stories, which provide the clearest indications for inferring the ostensible primary readership. The first type of story relates to the conflicts that arise when Afro-American students desegregate white schools. The second concerns the efforts of white children to cope with prejudice and discrimination against newfound Black friends. The third focuses on Blacks and whites working together within the "system" to effect change. The final story involves individual Black children learning to be friends with whites. A list of social conscience books used in this survey is presented at the end of the chapter.

Story #1: School Desegregation—Marching into the Lion's Den

Since this survey includes only two examples of the school desegregation story, both will be summarized. *The Empty Schoolhouse* (Carlson, 1965) is the story of Lullah Royall, one of the first Black children to attend an elementary school in a Louisiana parish. She wants to attend in order to spend more time with Oralee, her white best friend. The desegregation of the school is met with brick throwing and bomb threats, and soon Lullah is the only child attending school, which is abandoned by the whole community, including Oralee. Outside agitators who have been stirring up trouble finally shoot Lullah in the ankle, bringing the rational local people to their senses. Order is restored, Oralee and Lullah make up, and school is resumed on a hopeful note.

Lions in the Way (Rodman, 1966) brings to mind the story of the desegregation of Little Rock's Central High School. Eight Afro-American students have been chosen to integrate a high school in Tennessee. They are met with hostility and violence, partly stirred up by outside agitators. Robby, the leader of the Black students, is treated particularly harshly. A white minister who had taken a moral stand in favor of integration is badly beaten, partially blinded, and hospitalized after walking to school with the Black students. His beating prods community leaders to accept their responsibility to maintain order, and school reopens, minus one of the Black students and with the cooperation of a white student leader who had at one time been Robby's good friend.

Story #2: "How to Behave When the Black Folks Move In," or "Guess Who's Coming to Dinner?"

In the second basic story, the protagonist is a white child or adolescent. This young person befriends a Black child, adolescent, or family who has recently moved into the white protagonist's com-

munity or social circle. The protagonist meets hostility and discovers racial prejudice among friends, neighbors, and parents.
The protagonist is able to convince the prejudiced adults and
young people to be at least tolerant of the Afro-Americans, and
the lives of all concerned are richer and sweeter. In one twist on
this theme, *Turn the Next Corner* (Alcock, 1969), it is the white
child who moves into a "changing neighborhood," but the other
elements are virtually the same.

Perhaps the summary of one book of this kind will serve as a
model. It is an exaggeration of all the worst qualities of such
books, but it does contain all the characterizing elements. The title,
Easy Does It (Wier, 1965), probably expresses one of the recurring
subthemes of these books: Easy does it; integration must be
handled in small steps—a hello now, a lunch next week, and so
forth. That is the advice of a police officer at a neighborhood
meeting, held because the neighborhood is disquieted when a
"colored" engineer and his family move in. The son, A.L. Rees,
who is exceptionally bright and an excellent baseball catcher, is
befriended by Chip, the white protagonist. When the neighbors,
led by Jerk-Eye Hatcher, are hostile to the Rees family, only Chip's
family and that of Kosher Cohen (Yes, the smartest boy in the
class!) do not take part in the hostilities. Later, Chip's mother
joins a boycott. Jerk-Eye Hatcher falsely accuses Mr. Rees of kill-
ing his dog, but Chip saves the day by telling the neighborhood
gathering the truth as he witnessed it. The policeman makes his
"easy does it" speech, and the next day A.L. invites Chip over to
meet his godfather, "Terrible Thomas, the Blackest and the Best"
pitcher in the major leagues, who is, predictably, Chip's idol.
Terrible Thomas gives out autographs and pitching tips, and the
team gives A.L. the key to the clubhouse.

Story #3: Doing It the Right Way—Working within the "System"

In the third basic story, a Black child or family, usually with the
aid of liberal whites, uses the "system"—peaceful marches, demon-
strations, or petitions—to achieve some goal, most often a new
home, although one of the books focuses on being sent to a better
school.

A New Home for Billy (Justus, 1966) has been placed in this
category because its author purports to suggest "the right way"
to go about facing integration, even though the book does not involve an organized protest. The book jacket reads, "As more and
more Negroes have to seek homes out of the old city ghettos, the
situation described in this book will have to be faced. She shows

how it can be done—the right way." Apparently, the right way in this case is for Blacks to first make an effort to help themselves (Billy's father agrees to fix up a shanty in which he can live rent free for a while), and then for whites to pitch in and help when the efforts of the Blacks are unsuccessful. (Billy's father, delayed by the weather and by priorities of building play equipment and of his job, sprains his ankle, and the neighbors pitch in to finish fixing up the shanty.)

Marchers for the Dream (Carlson, 1969) is perhaps more typical. Another housing integration story, it suggests that the right way is the way of Martin Luther King, Jr. Bethany and her great-grand-mother go to Washington, D.C., to live in Resurrection City for a brief time when they have to vacate their apartment, which is in the path of the urban renewal wrecking ball. Because of discrimination, they have been unable to locate affordable housing. Upon their return from D.C., Grandma decides to picket City Hall. She is joined by her family and by others concerned about discrimination. After a few days, a white man offers to rent them a house in a white neighborhood, and the story ends on a hopeful note when a blond girl in the new neighborhood speaks to Bethany.

The portrait of Grandma is a positive one—strong and determined. The description of Resurrection City is well done, and there are other points to recommend the book. Unfortunately, there is still the obligatory Afro-wearing militant in the tent city spouting antiwhite slogans, and the incredibly naive image of a twelve-year-old girl, who has been held in Mississippi jails twice, running around saying, "Oh, my Gee," and hoping to be arrested.

Story #4: Learning to Get Along with Whites

In the fourth story, a Black protagonist is thrown unwillingly into contact with whites. Usually, the Black child, assuming the white child will be hostile, is hostile to the white child, apparently on the theory that the best defense is a good offense. In almost every case, the white protagonist has some personal problem—divorced parents, feelings of rejection—which explains his or her behavior.

One variation of this story, *Sound of Sunshine, Sound of Rain* (Heide, 1970), is the story of a blind Black boy who is befriended by a balloon man, Abram. It is the boy's sister who sees the world through hostile lenses—she sees trees as caged, while the balloon man sees them as protected, like a baby in a crib. Abram says, "All colors are the same. Colors are just on the outside. They're just covers for things, like blankets."

Another book with a slight twist on the basic story is *Sail, Calypso!* (Jones, 1968). While the conflict between the two boys who are the major characters is not racially motivated, the book has been placed in this category because racial differences are alluded to, and the Black boy must come to recognize the problems being faced by his white friend.

Both *The Good Morrow* (Norris, 1971) and *The Almost Year* (Randall, 1971) present Black girls with chips on their shoulders, expecting to be disliked and striking out first. The unnamed narrator of *The Almost Year* is so hostile that she raises a poltergeist, so perhaps her story is not realistic fiction. She has come to spend an academic year with the Mallorys while Aunt Cyd goes to a "live-in" job. Aunt Cyd had been Mrs. Mallory's nurse when her youngest child was born, and they had maintained a friendship for five years.

In *The Good Morrow*, a book for younger children, Josie goes to camp and clashes with Nancy, a white girl who is feeling rejected by her parents and who takes her feelings out on Josie. Josie, apprehensive about the new experience, thinks Nancy dislikes her because she is Black. Both girls learn to look beneath the surface. Actually, Nancy knows all along that Josie was just afraid. It is Josie who must come to understand Nancy's problem.

Distinguishing Characteristics of the Social Conscience Books

As one reads the social conscience books, one becomes aware of certain recurring elements—some stock characters, some stereotypes, some attitudes expressed by characters or narrators, even some episodes—that together suggest whether the book is intended to mirror an Afro-American life experience or whether the author is even aware of its existence. These elements also suggest the perspective from which the author seems to view Afro-Americans, the preconceptions that appear to form the base on which an author builds a story. In the following pages, the most common of those recurring elements are discussed.

The White Villain

In the school desegregation books, the white villain is the "outside agitator"; and in some of the "guess who's coming to dinner" books, someone who lives in the community. But the stock villain is usually a male and often of low socioeconomic status, as indicated by his nonstandard speech. In *The Empty Schoolhouse*, for example, there are two such men: one, "flat headed with a red face and a long neck," the other with a "lumpy nose and puffy eyes. His top teeth poked over his bottom lip like an alligator's." In *Easy Does It*, he is Jerk-Eye Hatcher, whose language includes such utterances as, "We ain't gettin' nowheres. . . . It don't work. . . . They ain't comin' out." In *The Other Side of the Fence* (Cone, 1967), he is Mr. Purdy, of the dirty Purdys. The point to be made about such characterizations is that they can lead readers to see racism as an aberration, common only to those who are undesirable in some other general ways, too; those who are mean, ugly, dirty, or possibly beneath one's notice socially. The outside agitator can conveniently disappear, leaving the impression that the good people of the community had only a momentary lapse brought on by the situation.

In fairness, it must be pointed out that many of the social conscience books also include prejudiced individuals as members of the protagonist's family (for example, *Iggie's House*, Blume, 1970, and *The Other Side of the Fence*), or as respected members of the community. By the end of the story, they are often beginning to lose their prejudices, or at least gaining some tolerance. If unreconciled, they conveniently move away. And at least one troublemaker, Mrs. Barringer in *Iggie's House*, is a woman. In any case, the concept of racism is seldom directly confronted in these books. It seems to be equated instead with prejudgment, which, unlike racism, may at times be susceptible to reason and experience with the prejudged object(s) or person(s).

Perpetuating Stereotypes: Images of Blacks

It seems that even in the late sixties some non-Afro-American writers lacked awareness that certain physical descriptions were likely to be objectionable because they had become part of the stereotyped image of Afro-Americans. For one example, there is the Black shiny face. Even *Lions in the Way*, which has much else to recommend it, describes the white minister's wife peering into the shiny Black face of her maid, Beulah. The shiny face is brown when it appears on Gussie Foster in *The Other Side of the Fence*. For another example, some of these books would imply that Black people have difficulty moving or standing in normal ways. Beulah "plodded" around the minister's house on flat feet. *Joe Bean* (Agle, 1967) demonstrates classically stereotyped behavior as Joe shifts from one foot to the other, clears his throat, and scratches his head before speaking. Luke Johnson, a Black physicist in

Stronger Than Hate (Baker, 1969), "shuffles" into a room to announce to a gathering a serious decision he has just made.

Henry Johnson, Luke's son in *Stronger Than Hate*, is, fortunately, unique as a character in these books. He seems drawn from old Charlie Chan movies featuring Mantan Moreland saying, "Feets, don't fail me now." Henry, who is about fifteen, has an extraordinary fear of whites. At one point, he runs to a cemetery to hide. "Move over dead people; here I come," he announces on arrival. Prior to his flight, he had "rolled his eyes pleadingly" from one white boy to another, begging, "Why don't you let me go home?" Later, when a friendly white girl discovers him hiding in the cemetery, he is moaning in fright, "What you want with this Black boy? I never done you no harm." This extraordinary fear leads to his death by drowning when he runs into the water to escape some hostile whites, even though he cannot swim.

Afro-American children are also portrayed as having extraordinary appetites. In *Lions in the Way*, Robby, the Black protagonist, fondly remembers that his erstwhile white friend Joel had had an insatiable appetite, "just like a colored kid's." An example of a "colored kid's" appetite is provided in *Joe Bean* when Joe eats his first meal in the home of a white family: "four sandwiches, three slices of cake, and countless glasses of lemonade." Joe is eleven years old.

The counter stereotype, the Super Negro, is also present in the social conscience books, most notably in *Easy Does It*. Eleven-year-old A.L. Rees is so smart that he is in the seventh grade at least a year ahead of his age mates. Besides, he is a terrific catcher. His father is an engineer, but his godfather is Terrible Thomas, who had "done something pretty big for his people" by becoming the best pitcher in the major leagues. In *A Question of Harmony* (Sprague, 1965), the Super Negro is Mel, who is both a talented violinist *and* a star halfback on his football team. The problem is that too often the Super Negro is made to seem acceptable only because of superiority to both Blacks and whites. Who could resist superdoctor Sidney Poitier on his way to a Nobel Prize in the film *Guess Who's Coming to Dinner?*

It may appear that the pointing out of such specific details is nitpicking and out of context. But it is precisely through such specific detail that image-makers cast the spells that make us see the world through their eyes. What is important is that even in the late sixties child readers were being presented images of Afro-Americans as, at best, uncomfortably different from other Americans, and, at worst, objects of ridicule.

Other Recurring Clichés

The Fatherless Home. Apparently, the writers of these books had been reading 1960s descriptions of the so-called disadvantaged. The single most frequently occurring phenomenon in the social conscience books is the absent Black father. In some cases, he has died; in others, he has simply disappeared. But there are enough fatherless Afro-American children in these books to cause one to wonder how Afro-Americans have managed to procreate and survive in a nearly manless society. More importantly, it raises questions about the implied willingness or ability of Afro-American men to be responsible members of their own families.

The Defeated, Hopeless Woman. Another Afro-American character who appears in a few of the social conscience books is the defeated, frightened person, usually a woman, who has given up and who discourages the young protagonists from pursuing their rights and their personal goals. In *A Question of Harmony*, the mother of Mel, the violin-playing halfback, tells him, "Mel, what are you trying to do, boy? . . . When there's any trouble, it's us [Blacks] that's making it. And getting it." Jeff, in *50,000 Names for Jeff* (Snyder, 1969), circulates a petition in spite of his illiterate mother's insistence that the system will not work for them. (She cannot even sign the petition until Jeff helps her write her name.) And in *Dead End School* (Coles, 1968), there is a meeting at which some people declare that since "Whitey" has all the power, Blacks cannot win; they should therefore be satisfied with what they have and live with it. (In that case, the answer of James's grandmother is to rely on prayer, another cliché that is common to some other books about Afro-Americans.) While frightened, defeated people do exist in Afro-American communities, in these books, which were among the first attempts to remedy the invisibility of the modern Afro-American child, it might have been better to omit such defeated characters unless their fear and sense of defeat could have been made plausible.

Black Language. For the most part, the Afro-Americans in the social conscience books speak standard English, or at least the same variety as that spoken by the non-Afro-American characters. Where attempts are made to indicate language variation, it is encouraging to note that the plantation dialect of an earlier era has virtually disappeared. What replaces it in these books is, typically, nonstandard English, though usually in contrast to the standard English of non-Afro-American characters. In *Joe Bean*, for instance, the white boy, Monk, says, "You'll be my captive audience." Joe replies, "I'm on probation, but I ain't no captive."

Clay, in *A Single Trail* (Rose, 1969), utters sentences like, "I ain't got no money." While the nonstandard English in itself is not objectionable, the tendency to use it to characterize only the Afro-Americans in contrast to others, suggests, given the low esteem in which nonstandard constructions are generally held, another uncomfortable difference between the Black and white characters.

Attitudes and Assumptions, Expressed and Implied

If you're white, all right; if you're brown, stick around; if you're black, stay back. This attitude is expressed in several of the social conscience books, often by a Black character. It suggests that beauty, and perhaps goodness, are determined by how closely one's physical characteristics resemble those of Euro-Americans. In *The Empty Schoolhouse*, Emma Royall informs us that her brother is handsome *in spite of* his dark skin and short hair, and that her sister and mother are pretty because of their lighter skin and long wavy hair. In *Lions in the Way*, the prettiest girl in the Black student group is the one with blue-gray eyes, a coffee-and-cream complexion, and shoulder-length hair. Mrs. Slager, in *Turn the Next Corner*, is described as a pretty woman, lighter in complexion than her son, Slugger. The most blatant examples come from *A New Home for Theresa* (Baum, 1968). Theresa is convinced that the blacker one is, the dumber one is. Since she is dark-skinned, she must be fairly close to idiocy. Theresa was very glad that she had been taught to straighten her hair, since she thought it took courage to wear nappy hair to school, to go around looking like an African. In the middle of her first night in a foster home, she is wakeful and turns on the light. "Maybe I've turned white now. I'd better look." It must be obvious that such an attitude, such an image of "Black is *not* beautiful," cannot be calculated to meet the literary needs of those of us whose complexion is closer to espresso than light coffee and whose hair is nappy and short. The message is, indeed, if you are Black, stay back.

Race Mixing Naturally Leads to Trouble. It is interesting that this assumption seems to underlie almost all of the social conscience books. In the "learning to get along with whites" subgroup, it is underplayed, although it is still present. In only one of the books, *Lions in the Way*, is there more than a superficial attempt by non-Afro-American characters or narrators to explore the origins of the negative attitudes and behavior of white characters.

Jerk-Eye Hatcher, in *Easy Does It*, does mention the devaluing of property, and that fear is also expressed in *Iggie's House* and *Stronger Than Hate*. At least one Afro-American character, the engineer in *Easy Does It*, suggests that whites' fear of change must be understood and given time to abate. But in book after book, the fact that whites will react negatively to the presence of Blacks is simply assumed. The impression is that the very "differentness" of Afro-Americans from Euro-Americans is sufficient cause for fear and hostility. *Turn the Next Corner* provides one of the clearest examples. Ritchie, a white boy who has moved into a "changing neighborhood" on the edge of the ghetto, makes friends with Slugger, who is Black. But Ritchie automatically assumes that his mother will not like his having a Black friend, so he hesitates to tell her. It is all right, it turns out, as long as he does not go west of Well Street where there are so many Blacks that riots could break out any time. Ritchie is also uncomfortable in his new school, since in addition to Negro and white children there are also Mexican-Americans, Puerto Ricans, and Chinese-Americans. Why, he even feels too well dressed! Ritchie does, however, feel comfortable in Slugger's apartment with Slugger and his parents; but when he wanders west of Well Street, that is different. There are so many Negroes there. Everyone is Black!

This assumption that the mere presence of Blacks is a problem in itself is a very basic flaw of the social conscience books. It permits the problem to be seen as "the Black problem." Further, it evades the issue of racism and leads to the implication that if white people can only learn to tolerate the presence of Blacks, with all their alien oddities, all will be well.

Patronizing and Paternalism. The social conscience books, unlike the melting pot books, recognize differences between Afro-Americans and others. However, the differences are frequently presented so as to make Afro-Americans appear quaint or exotic. This quasi-foreignness then becomes an excuse for paternalism or patronizing on the part of the non-Afro-American characters, or the narrator, or, by implication, the author.

One example of this kind of attitude appears in *A New Home for Theresa*. Theresa's social worker, a fat white woman who "fills up a room with friendliness," says, "I think that being born a Negro in this country does something harmful to a child. He feels inferior, and because he feels this way he can't work as well as the child who feels good about himself." If the mere fact of being born "a Negro" does the harm, then all is lost, since that condition is not amenable to change. It is, rather, the experiences and conditions to which Black people are subjected that cause the harm, which is a very different matter. But it is that pathological perspective on the problem that permits Theresa to wake up in the middle of the night, hoping she has turned white.

A New Home for Theresa provides another example of patronizing attitudes. There is an implication that Afro-Americans, even though the plot calls for many of them to have the wherewithal to buy suburban homes, are totally unfamiliar with and awed by typical suburban homes and their furnishings. When Theresa arrives at the home of her new foster parents, which is a middle-class Long Island apartment, she is so impressed with the relative material wealth she sees there that she assumes the apartment must belong to a white woman for whom her foster mother works. Theresa had been poor, but, even so, her reaction is exaggerated. Joe Bean, too, is overly impressed with the home of his benefactors, though this is perhaps not implausible since the home is a rather large, horsey, Maryland estate. In *Stronger Than Hate*, the Afro-Americans who have moved from the city and are temporarily living in tents are awed by the sight of the home of the whites who befriend them. Felix, a young Black child who had apparently been living in a tenement, does not recognize a faucet he sees in the house. Mrs. Rees, in *Easy Does It*, is impressed by the cleanliness of Chip's house. This Black wife of an engineer remarks that Chip's mother must be an excellent housekeeper and recalls how her own family used to leave crumbs on the floor for the chickens to clean up.

If Afro-Americans in these books are overawed by typical middle-class homes, then it is not surprising that they are grateful for accommodations that would be considered unsuitable for most other people. One of the women living in an orange tent in a field in *Stronger Than Hate* declares, "It's so peaceful and pleasant here, I don't really care if I find a home or not." The new home for Billy in the book of that title is a rundown shanty that apparently is barely habitable. But with a coat of paint and a bit of fixing up, the house makes Billy's mother so happy she wants to hug it.

One of the most blatant examples of a paternalistic attitude is found in *Stronger Than Hate*. In this story, five Afro-American families have moved into tents in a field until they can find homes. When Mrs. Ferris, the white co-owner of the land, goes to visit the families, she is invited to tea. Upon meeting Mrs. Ferris, one of the Black women "giggles and shakes her head wonderingly." She also "ducks her head and apologizes" for having said her husband should be referred to as Mr. Mann. But almost immediately, the Black women confide in Mrs. Ferris information that no group of families in similar circumstances would be likely to give so freely and openly and quickly to a stranger—who among them is scared, who does not like whom, who is helping them, and so forth. Their conversation is an obvious story device for getting the issues out, but it is implausible that in the given situation the mere friendly presence of a white woman would elicit such giggling and open trust.

In the "getting along with whites" books, there is often an implied comparison between the problems of the Black child and some problems of the white child. For example, Nancy, in *The Good Morrow*, is feeling rejected by her pregnant mother, while Josie clearly has a loving mother; in *The Almost Year*, the white teenagers have problems, too—Holly is not popular and Gary is a lousy ball player. The problems of these white children, like real-life problems of that nature, are important to them. But to equate these fears with the pervasive effects of racism is to minimize those effects on the lives of Black children and to suggest that their fears and apprehensions are totally unfounded and inexplicable. True, Black children also need to learn to judge individuals on their own merits, but one cannot forget that Black children know that their being Black evokes many negative reactions from people whom they have never seen before. In the face of that experience, their behavior is hardly inexplicable.

Throughout the social conscience books are other examples, though not quite so prevalent, of other objectionable clichés—the long-suffering, uncomplaining Black; the loyal and subservient Black. The cumulative effect of all these features is to suggest that the Afro-Americans in these books are viewed from a perspective that is at once ethnocentric and paternalistic. In the final analysis, the social conscience books fail to change the world because the perspective from which they are written permits readers to maintain their original racial views without challenge.

Conclusion

The social conscience books, in general, "may mean good, but they do so doggone poor!" Their publication in the late sixties helped to increase the visibility of the Afro-American child in the world of children's books. Their topics were timely, highlighting prominent social issues of concern to everyone. On the other hand, the literary quality of many of them is poor enough to suggest that had they not been timely, they might not have been published at all.

From an Afro-American perspective, the best of the social conscience books are those that are set outside the confines of an Afro-American family and that do not have a strong moralizing emphasis on the behavior of a white protagonist. Of the two school desegregation books, *The Empty Schoolhouse*, which won a Child Study Association Award, fails because its presentation of Lullah and her family is lacking in sociocultural awareness. On the other hand, *Lions in the Way* is long enough and complex enough to present a number of characters, both Black and white, representing a number of different views on the issue. The fact that the story covers just one extraordinary week of crisis permits a number of formal and informal meetings, during which various positions can be expressed. It permits Reverend Logan to place the issue in a historical context and to speak of choices incumbent on whites in positions of power. The book avoids the happy-ever-after ending so typical of the social conscience books. While there is hope, it is also clear that there has been no miraculous reversal of racial attitudes. The community leaders see the need to maintain an orderly society, and they will do what they must. Thus, even with its flaws, *Lions in the Way*, which also tells a good story, is among the best of the social conscience books. However, it is out of print as of the 1978-1979 edition of *Books in Print*.

The "guess who's coming to dinner" books are tainted by heavy moralizing; almost all are tainted by patronization, paternalism, and tokenism. Three of the eight, *Stronger Than Hate*, *The Other Side of the Fence*, and *c/o Arnold's Corners* (Newton, 1974), are apparently out of print. *Easy Does It* and *A Question of Harmony*, two of the worst books, were still listed in the 1978-1979 *Books in Print*.

The "using the system" books, all of which are in print at this writing, receive mixed reviews. *A New Home for Billy*, in addition to its sociocultural problems, reads like a poorly written primer. *A New Home for Theresa* perpetuates the idea that there is something pathological about being Black. On the other hand, most of these books have the virtue of showing Blacks working to solve their own problems, even while they place much faith in the very institutions that have been used to create the conditions the Blacks are fighting against.

The "learning to get along with whites" books are sometimes preachy and are insensitive enough to equate racism with some personal problem such as inattentive parents or lack of popularity among peers. Those are very real problems for some children, but they are very different from the problems caused by the effects of individual and institutional racism. Thus, the issues are over-simplified.

In general, while they might have been a step in the right direction and served some useful purpose at the time of their writing, the social conscience books deserve a long and relatively undisturbed rest on the library shelves.

The Social Conscience Books

School Desegregation—Marching into the Lion's Den

Carlson, Natalie Savage. *The Empty Schoolhouse.* New York: Harper and Row, 1965. (Gr. 2-6)*

Rodman, Bella. *Lions in the Way.* Chicago: Follett, 1966. (Gr. 7-up) O.P.**

"How to Behave When the Black Folks Move In"

Alcock, Gudrun. *Turn the Next Corner.* New York: Lothrop, Lee and Shepard, 1969. (Gr. 4-6)

Baker, Elizabeth. *Stronger Than Hate.* Boston: Houghton Mifflin, 1969. (Gr. 7-up) O.P.

Blume, Judy. *Iggie's House.* New York: Dell, 1970. (Gr. 4-7)

Brodsky, Mimi. *The House at Twelve Rose Street.* New York: Abelard Schuman, 1966. (Gr. 4-6)

Cone, Molly. *The Other Side of the Fence.* Boston: Houghton Mifflin, 1967. (Gr. 3-7) O.P.

Newton, Suzanne. *c/o Arnold's Corners.* Philadelphia: Westminster Press, 1974. (Gr. 4-6) O.P.

Sprague, Gretchen. *A Question of Harmony.* New York: Dodd, Mead and Co., 1965. (Gr. 7-up)

Wier, Ester. *Easy Does It.* New York: Vanguard Press, 1965. (Gr. 4-6)

Doing It the Right Way—Working within the "System"

Baum, Betty. *A New Home for Theresa.* New York: Alfred A. Knopf, 1968. (Gr. 4-8)

Carlson, Natalie Savage. *Marchers for the Dream.* New York: Harper and Row, 1969. (Gr. 4-7)

---

*There can be no hard and fast designations of grade levels for literature. However, for the sake of convenience, I have included grade-level designations from the 1979-1980 *Books in Print* as an estimate of difficulty. For books that are out of print, I have given my own estimates.
**O.P. = Out of Print. The title was not listed in the 1979–1980 *Books in Print* and is presumed to be out of print.

Coles, Robert. *Dead End School.* Boston: Little, Brown and Co., 1968. (Gr. 3-7)

Justus, May. *A New Home for Billy.* New York: Hastings House, 1966. (Gr. 2-4)

Snyder, Anne. *50,000 Names for Jeff.* New York: Holt, Rinehart and Winston, 1969. (Gr. 1-4)

Learning to Get Along with Whites

Agle, Nan Hayden. *Joe Bean.* New York: Seabury Press, 1967. (Gr. 3-6)

Heide, Florence. *Sound of Sunshine, Sound of Rain.* New York: Parents Magazine Press, 1970. (Gr. K-3)

Jones, Adrienne. *Sail, Calypso!* Boston: Little, Brown and Co., 1968. (Gr. 4-7)

Norris, Gunilla B. *The Good Morrow.* New York: Atheneum, 1971. (Gr. 3-7)

Randall, Florence. *The Almost Year.* New York: Atheneum, 1971. (Gr. 5-9)

Rose, Karen. *A Single Trail.* New York: Follett, 1969. (Gr. 5-8)

3 Conjuring in the Melting Pot

You can hide the fire, but what you goin' to do with the smoke?

Traditional Afro-American Saying

Concurrent with the publication of the social conscience books but continuing into the late seventies is a second group of books about Afro-American children that concentrates on the idea that people are people are people. . . . They echo the theme of the social conscience book by Florence Parry Heide, *Sound of Sunshine, Sound of Rain*: "All colors are the same. Colors are just on the outside. They're just covers for things, like blankets." The implication is that Americans have all been placed in the proverbial melting pot and have emerged homogeneous and culturally interchangeable.

On some level, all good literature speaks to that which is universal in each of us, and to that degree the melting pot books can be considered good literature. Some of them are, indeed, quite worthwhile and deservedly popular. However, Americans have not been homogenized in the melting pot and are not all culturally interchangeable like the standardized components that make mass production possible. In spite of that fact, the distinguishing characteristics of the melting pot books are that they not only make a point of recognizing our universality, but that they also make a point of ignoring our differences.

Actually, the melting pot books ignore all differences *except* physical ones: skin color and other racially related physical features. The result is that the majority of them are picture books. The format of a picture book, and such other specifications of that genre as length constraints, permit the recurring phenomenon that most readily distinguishes the melting pot books from the social conscience books and the culturally conscious books—without the illustrations one would have no way of knowing that the story was about an Afro-American child. That is, nothing in the text itself identifies the Afro-American child as such, and even if the illustrator had chosen to give that child a different racial/ ethnic identity, the text could have remained unchanged.

Obviously, then, the melting pot books, in contrast to the social conscience books, do not concern themselves with racial prejudice, discrimination, or conflict. Nor do they project any distinctly Afro-American experiences or traditions. Their topics and themes are the same as those of other realistic picture books for young children—friendships, family relationships, familiar everyday experiences. Their diversity makes it difficult to place them in a small number of discrete categories having common themes and topics. What seems to bind these books into a single group is their focus on integration (not to be confused with the desegregation of the social conscience books), either within the books or within the mainstream of American children's literature and culture. Thus, the forty melting pot books used in this survey have been divided, for discussion purposes, into three major categories. Two groups, representing about half the melting pot books, are integrated in the sense that they have both Black and white major characters. The third group have all-Black or nearly all-Black casts of characters who are firmly set in the mold of mainstream American cultural values.

Afro-Americans in Stories about Non-Afro-Americans

As with the social conscience books, one group of the melting pot books, though listed in bibliographies of books about Blacks, actually have non-Afro-American children as main characters. In some cases, the books are about whites, with Afro-Americans playing some important role. In others, the story is about the relationship between a white child and a Black one, but the story is presented as seen through the eyes of the white child.

Perhaps the most extreme example in the survey of Black characters as backdrop to a white character's story is *A Certain Small Shepherd* (Caudill, 1965), which is a modern recalling of the Christmas story. Jamie, a white six-year-old, has never talked. A first grader, he was all set to be a shepherd in the school Christmas play, but it was canceled by a snow storm. The storm also forced a young couple to seek shelter with his family. The couple is housed in the church, where they give birth to a child during the night. On Christmas morning, the miracle of birth is augmented by a second miracle for Jamie. The couple, according to the illustrations, is Black.

Another picture book, *Sabrina* (Alexander, 1971), presents a white girl, Sabrina, who wants to give away her odd name and be called Susan. Black twins Amy and Susan argue over who is to get the "princess name." The teacher, who is also Black, lets Sabrina decide.

A third book of this type, *Luke Was There* (Clymer, 1973), is one of the few melting pot books in this survey that is not a picture book. It is the story of Julius, a white boy who has been placed in a child care center. Luke is the Black social worker and conscientious objector on whom Julius depends for stability and support.

In all three of these books, the Black characters are essential to the white characters' stories, but the fact that they are Black is irrelevant. That fact neither enhances nor detracts from the story itself, although in *A Certain Small Shepherd*, the fact that the couple is Black seems to add to the drama of the story. The twins in *Sabrina* could as easily have been blond and blue-eyed. Luke is a better developed character, but he too could as easily have been a blond, blue-eyed rock for Julius to lean on. These books are not in any real sense Afro-American literature.

Four other books in this group concern friendships between Black and white children. These are the "me and ＿＿" books: *Me and Arch and the Pest* (Durham, 1970); *Steffie and Me* (Hoffman, 1970); *Jennifer, Hecate, MacBeth, William McKinley and Me, Elizabeth* (Konigsburg, 1967); and *The Toothpaste Millionaire* (Merrill, 1972). In all four cases, the narrator, the "me" in three of the titles, is a white child.

Steffie and Me is a picture book; the other three, along with *Luke Was There* and *Project Cat* (Burchardt, 1966), are the only nonpicture books in the melting pot category of the survey. They are all illustrated, however, and so again permit the burden of evidence of the Black identity of the narrator's friend to fall on the pictures.

Actually, in *The Toothpaste Millionaire* and *Me and Arch and the Pest*, reference is made in the text to the Black characters' racial identity. In fact, *Me and Arch and the Pest* resembles some of the social conscience books in that Bit, the white main character, has parents who come from Georgia and, apparently as a consequence of that fact, do not like "the colored." They are stereotypes of poor white southerners. However, unlike the social conscience books, racial conflict is not the focus of Bit's story, and he does not bring his parents or community to see the error of their ways. Instead, he and his friend Arch, who is described as having skin the color of light coffee, have an adventure involving a dognapping racket and the rescue of Pest, the German shepherd who has adopted the boys. *Me and Arch and the Pest* also resembles the culturally conscious books in that it makes a feeble attempt to represent Arch as a speaker of hip Black English: "Thing to do is just open your mouth, baby, and let it roll out." But in any case, this is only secondarily Arch's story; it is primarily Bit's story, and since its focus is not on racial conflict but on interracial friendship, it has been placed with the melting pot books.

The main character in *The Toothpaste Millionaire* is twelve-year-old Rufus Mayflower. (I wonder what the 1980 census has revealed about the number of Black boys born in the last twenty years who have been named Rufus.) Having decided that seventy-nine cents is an extravagant price for a tube of toothpaste, Rufus becomes a millionaire by making and developing his own, which he sells initially for three cents a tube. The story is narrated by Kate, Rufus's helper, a shareholder, and member of the board of his corporation. Kate, who is white, does mention, in a self-congratulatory way, that Rufus is Black, as is Hector, the manager they hire. But again, this is neither a social conscience book nor a culturally conscious book; it is a comedy, a spoof on business practices, and if it is to be enjoyed, it requires a willing suspension of disbelief in any case.

The other two "me and ___" books fit more neatly into the melting pot. *Steffie and Me* tells the story of a friendship between two girls. Steffie is Black, the narrator is not. But only the pictures say "for sure." *Steffie and Me* has the virtue of being the sole "me and ___" book that presents a truly integrated social setting in the sense that integration extends to home and family, with both girls visiting each other's homes, and the friendship apparently is based on mutual respect and affection.

In contrast, in the Newbery Honor Book *Jennifer, Hecate, MacBeth, William McKinley and Me, Elizabeth*, Jennifer, who is Elizabeth's Black friend, dominates their friendship by making Elizabeth an apprentice witch. Jennifer is apparently the only Black child in her school and community. She and Elizabeth sustain their secret and imaginative friendship, centering on witchery, from Halloween until spring. Thus, Jennifer's family remains anonymous, and Elizabeth's parents do not meet Jennifer until spring. It is Elizabeth whose life is reflected; Jennifer is fascinating and bright, and the story is very well written, but the witch game allows no opportunity for Jennifer's home life to play a role in the story, and so she is seen in relative isolation.

This device, placing Black characters in situations external to home, family, and Black community, is characteristic of this group of melting pot books. It is one of the means by which authors and illustrators can create books including Black characters yet can be relieved of the task of providing the specific details that suggest an awareness of sociocultural differences between Afro-American and Euro-American children.

Given the non-Black protagonists, and the fact that these stories are told from their point of view, one might infer that the primary audience for this group of melting pot books is also non-Black. The intention seems to be to integrate the fictional world of white American children. The point seems to be that interracial encounters and friendships can and do occur naturally and without racial conflict.

Afro-American Children in Integrated Settings

A second group of melting pot books focuses on personal problems or experiences of Black children, unrelated to racial conflict but taking place in racially integrated settings. These, too, focus in most cases on experiences outside the family circle. They are almost all picture books, and the pictures are the only means of identifying the characters as Black.

The fact that the single thread holding this group together is their presentation of Black children in an integrated society results in a wide range of topics and themes. The following are some examples that demonstrate this variety.

Two of the books, somewhat like the "me and ____" books, present close interracial friendships. They are all reminiscent of the pioneering work by Lorraine and Jerrold Beim, *Two Is a Team*, (New York: Harcourt, Brace, and World, 1945) which was the first picture book to present such a democratic friendship. They differ from the "me and ____" books in that the point of view is not exclusively that of the white child. *The Valentine Box* (Lovelace, 1966) actually focuses on the initiation of such a friendship. Janice, a Black fifth-grader, has moved to Oak Grove from the city. She is the only Black child in her class and has been too shy to approach Margaret, with whom she would like to be friends. On Valentine's Day, although she has had the time and energy to make valentines for the other children, she is afraid they have not done so for her, since she is so new and has made no friends. On the way back to school after lunch, she helps Margaret collect her dropped and wind-scattered valentines, and a new interracial friendship is launched. Interestingly, Janice is not at all apprehensive about racial prejudices, which would be a much more plausible explanation for her fear of not receiving valentines than her newness. It is also implausible that her teacher had not made certain that Janice was included on the valentine list, since Janice must have either had time to make *some* friends or had access to such a list in order to make valentines for other children. In other words, the story seems contrived merely to make a point about interracial friendships.

The main characters in *Gabrielle and Selena* (Desbarats, 1968) have long been friends; in fact, they are like sisters. When one day they decide to adopt each other's identities, they each go off to the other's houses to spend the night. Both sets of parents appear to go along with the game, but they trick the girls into giving it up by pretending that their daughter likes to eat and do things she does not. The girls discover that they have been tricked as they meet halfway between houses on their way to their respective homes. Rudman (1976) has raised some questions worth thinking about in relationship to this book—why girls who are as close as sisters would not know more about each other's likes and dislikes, and why their parents were unwilling to go along with their game. Again, the point seems to be that "color blind" interracial friendships can and do exist.

Three other books in this group concern the need to get along in school. *Shawn Goes to School* (Breinburg, 1973) is about Shawn's introduction to nursery school and overcoming his fearfulness. *Leroy, OOPS* (Glasser, 1971) tells how Leroy, with the help of a teacher, learns to channel his energy in positive directions. *Willaby* (Isadora, 1977) continues the "school story" pattern as Willaby, who likes to draw, has a hard time with the class get-well card for her teacher.

Other books focus on a fairly wide range of topics. *Project Cat* (Burchardt, 1966) resembles the social conscience, "working within the system" books in that Betsy and her friends literally take their problem to city hall and place it in the hands of the mayor and the city council. However, their problem is not discrimination against Blacks, but a "no pet" rule in the housing project that places in peril the survival of a pregnant cat and her kittens-to-be. Other books concern learning to tie one's shoe (*When Shoes Eat*

Socks, Klimowicz, 1971), getting lost on the subway (*Nicholas*, Kempner, 1968), learning what it takes to be considered big (*Hooray for Jasper*, Horvath, 1966), and making friends with neighbors in an apartment building (*Fat Ernest*, Weil, 1973). One book, *City Rhythms* (Grifalconi, 1965), is actually a celebration of the city and its sounds, joined by a rhythm band of instruments from the junk yard.

Unique among the books in the survey and perhaps among books with important Afro-American characters is *Bobo's Dream* (Alexander, 1970). It is unique because it features a Black child in a textless book. The Bobo of the title is a dachshund who belongs to a young Black boy. After the boy retrieves Bobo's bone from the huge dog that has taken it from him, Bobo dreams that he returns the favor by helping the boy and his friends retrieve their football from the big bullies who, in Bobo's dream, have taken it from them. He wakes from his dream brave enough to intimidate the big dog when he returns. *Bobo's Dream* is unique, too, because it is actually the dog's story. One could quarrel about how realistic it is, but the fantasy is in the dream. It does present a Black child in an integrated setting, though only the butcher and one friend are white.

The fact that the point of view in these integrated books has shifted from that of white characters, as in the first group, to that of Black characters invites the speculation that the authors may have had in mind a primary readership of Black children. On the other hand, the fact that white children also play major roles and the deliberate focus on integrated settings may mean that the primary readership was expected to be integrated, too.

While the point of view in this group of books is usually that of the Black child, there is no attempt to present an Afro-American perspective. As with melting pot books in general, the idea that such a perspective exists seems not to have been taken into account.

Black Children, Black Families

The last group of melting pot books are those that include only Black major characters. A few, such as *What Mary Jo Shared* (Udry, 1966), also include white characters, but they are the reverse of the first group of melting pot books in that the white characters are background characters in the Black child's story. Like almost all the other melting pot books, only the pictures indicate that these are stories about Black children.

These books, too, are diverse in theme and topic, reflecting some of the range of subjects to be found in children's realistic fiction in general. There are stories, for instance, about divorce, other family relationships, animals, school, and coping with one's emotions. Others involve such everyday experiences as walking to school alone or getting oneself out of predicaments. All are picture books for young children. Some examples follow.

Two of these books concern animals. *Mississippi Possum* (Miles, 1965) actually alternates point of view from that of a possum to that of Rosemary Jackson, whose family the possum adopts. Both the possum and the Jacksons flee a flood and eventually return home, where the possum takes up residence in a log at the back of the Jackson's home. A possum also figures in *Joey's Cat* (Burch, 1969). The title cat, who is not permitted to be a house cat, has kittens in the garage. When the protective mother cat starts bringing her kittens into the house, Joey and his father discover that she has been frightened by a possum. After the possum is removed, Joey's mother decides to relax her "no cats in the house" rule to let the kittens stay.

Two books involve the relationship between girls and their divorced fathers. In *Daddy* (Caines, 1977), Windy enjoys spending Saturdays with her father and his new wife. In *Eliza's Daddy* (Thomas, 1976), Eliza is curious about her father's "other" family, and when she finally gathers the courage to ask to meet them, it turns out to be a pleasant experience. There are small details in both these books that suggest they might well be placed in the culturally conscious group: a reference to sweet potato pie, a father who calls his daughter "Baby." But otherwise, they fit quite well into the melting pot group.

The best known, and probably the best of these books, are those that involve children and their experiences and relationships within a family unit. Three examples may help characterize the group. While most such books feature solidly middle-class families, *Evan's Corner* (Hill, 1967) features a family of eight who live in two rooms. Evan needs his own space in the crowded apartment, but after his understanding mother allows him to choose his own corner and after he fixes it up to his satisfaction, he discovers he also has a need to reach out to help someone else. In *What Mary Jo Shared*, Mary Jo, after many unsuccessful attempts, finally decides on an ideal "item" to share during "share and tell" time at school—her father. In *Sam* (Scott, 1967), the main character, Sam, feels useless and rejected when his family is too involved in their own activities to bother with him, but then his mother finds just the right job for him.

Probably the most famous books of this type are the "Peter" books by Ezra Jack Keats: *The Snowy Day* (1962), *Whistle for Willie* (1964), *Peter's Chair* (1967), *A Letter to Amy* (1968), *Goggles!* (1969), *Hi, Cat!* (1970), *Pet Show* (1972). *The Snowy Day* was the first winner of the Caldecott Medal with a Black child as a major character, and on that account was a landmark book. It features Peter in a solitary but satisfying romp in the snow. It was followed by the others, all featuring Peter, his dog Willie, and, as Peter grew older, Archie and other neighborhood friends. The urban setting probably added to the books' appeal, since there had been far too few positive books set in unambiguous city surroundings and since there was a demand in the sixties for "urban literature."

This third group of melting pot books is a transition between the social conscience books and the culturally conscious books. They are not especially concerned with racial integration but present Black children within the context of their families and neighborhoods. They are the books that are most often described as being "universal" in their appeal to all readers. This universality, however, seems to be achieved in a rather facile manner, by viewing Afro-Americans with a tunnel vision that permits only one part of the duality of growing up Afro-American to be seen at a time.

Analyzing the Melting Pot Books

If the melting pot books assume a kind of cultural homogeneity for their subjects, it is likely that the same assumption applies to their presumed primary audience; melting pot books are not only about Any Child, they are written for Any Reader. It has already been pointed out that they are not intended to reflect any distinct Afro-American cultural experience. The third issue underlying this survey is that of perspective. As with the social conscience books, the general perspective of the melting pot books is best viewed through those elements, features, and characteristics that seem to recur throughout the books.

Distinguishing Features of the Melting Pot Books

Not surprisingly, in the melting pot books we are spared many of the worst features of the social conscience books—the moralizing, most of the paternalism, the recurrent negative images. Much of this is because the melting pot books deliberately ignore racial and subcultural differences in their texts. However, the melting pot books do share some features of their own.

Nuclear Families

The fatherless families of the social conscience books have been replaced, where families are included, by nuclear families. There are still one or two fatherless families—*Nicholas* and *Big Cowboy Western* (Scott, 1965)—but for the most part, the Black children in the melting pot books have responsible fathers present in the home.

Many of these nuclear families are middle class. In *Sam*, Sam's father sits at a desk, wearing a shirt and tie and reading the *New York Times*, his typewriter nearby. In *What Mary Jo Shared*, Mary Jo's father is an English teacher who enjoys reading, writing, and sailing. Joey's father in *Joey's Cat* is a policeman. The two divorced fathers seem solidly middle class, too.

Some families are less well off financially, but not because of absent fathers. Evan's family in *Evan's Corner* has six children in a two-room apartment. His mother works as a cleaning woman. Betsy in *Project Cat* lives in what seems to be a low-income housing project (even though the children seem to have ample money to spend on cat food), but both parents are present in her home.

The nuclear family is the model middle-class American family, although the rising divorce rate suggests that fewer and fewer such families exist. Thus, it is to be expected that books appearing to view American society as homogeneous would concentrate on the family structure assumed to be most representative of that society. While some of the focus on nuclear families may have been a response to criticisms that the woman-led Black family had become a stereotype, it is just as likely that much of it resulted from the desire to present a norm. In any case, these nuclear families provided a counter to, or perhaps an alternative to, the fatherless social conscience books. It remained, however, for the culturally conscious books to include another structure common to Afro-American experience—the extended family. In all the melting pot books in the survey, only one, *Hooray for Jasper*, includes a grandfather.

Language and Dialogue

The ignoring of subcultural differences, the mark of the melting pot books, also is implicit in the language the characters speak. With the notable exception of Arch in *Me and Arch and the Pest*, all the Afro-Americans in the melting pot books are speakers of standard English. There are one or two strange sounding sentences, such as "I'd mighty much like to earn enough to buy a turtle" from *Evan's Corner*, and "What for you crying, little boy?" from *When Shoes Eat Socks*. But while these are not necessarily standard English, they are not necessarily Black English either. Some of the dialogue seems somewhat sterile and stilted, given the age of the speakers. "That's *my* book, and you're not to touch it" may not be the way many ten- or eleven-year-old boys would express that sentiment to a younger brother. The point is, however, that the absence of Black English is another indicator of the assumption of homogeneity that marks the melting pot books.

Specific Details

Here and there throughout the melting pot books are small and seemingly innocuous details suggesting, in spite of the color-blind quality of the books, some nonvisual clues to or hints about the Black characters' racial identity. Some melting pot books have even been criticized for visually presenting perceived stereotypes. The portrayal of Peter's mother in *The Snowy Day*, for instance, was criticized because the woman is fat and wears a bright house dress, reminiscent of the fat Black "mammies" of plantation stereotypes.

Nothing so obvious appears in the texts, but a few details did raise some questions. For example, how common are names like Jasper and Rufus among modern American boys? Is there an association between those names and Blacks? If Rufus Mayflower, the toothpaste millionaire, had been white, would he have had a different name? For another example, the melting pot books vary in their use of terms of address for parents. It is interesting to speculate on whether an author's use of "Ma and Pa," "Mother and Father," "Mom and Dad," or "Mama and Daddy" is related to social or cultural associations. In a third example, given the association of watermelon with plantation stereotypes of Blacks, is it significant that Jennifer of *Jennifer, Hecate, MacBeth, William McKinley and Me, Elizabeth* chooses watermelon as the thing she will stop eating as part of her witching game with Elizabeth? If Jennifer had not been Black, would it have been cantaloupe? Even when authors make deliberate attempts at racial color blindness, the ultimate question is, are they sometimes influenced by some unconscious, internalized images of Afro-Americans partially resulting from the negative images of the past?

Illustrations

Since so many of the melting pot books are picture books and rely on the illustrations to indicate that characters are Black, it is important to examine and discuss some of the illustrations. Afro-Americans range in physical appearance from very pale to very dark and display facial features and hair textures on a spectrum from what is usually described as Negroid to what is usually described as Caucasian. The melting pot books seem to portray almost the entire range. Closest to the Caucasian end of the spectrum are *Project Cat* and *Hooray for Jasper*, which were both illustrated by Fermin Rocker. His Black characters are rather ambiguously shaded gray, and his females look rather European in face and hair. Jasper's mother wears a bun on top of her head, while Betsy's hair flies out behind her as she runs. The Black males in these books, however, do appear to have short, Afro-type hair. Interestingly, neither book is listed in the 1979-1980 edition of *Books in Print*. By the end of the sixties, there was a demand for unambiguously Black characters in books about Black kids.

On the other hand, many of the melting pot books were illustrated by some of the best-known illustrators of children's books, and often it is their artwork that makes a book special. Symeon Shimin, Janice May Udry, Ann Grifalconi, Martha Alexander, Evaline Ness, and Ezra Jack Keats are among the well-known illustrators who have created attractive, unambiguously Black images of Afro-American children. Three of them have won Caldecott awards, though only one was for a book about an Afro-American child. Their melting pot books reflect the kind of care and sensitivity one might expect from artists of such high repute.

It should be pointed out that only a few of the illustrators of melting pot books—Errol Lloyd, Moneta Barnett, Lee Jack Morton, Richard Lewis—are themselves Black. Ray Prather, another Black artist represented in the melting pot books, is one of the few Black author/illustrators currently being published who both write and illustrate their own books. Since all the authors of the social conscience books and almost all of the authors of the melting pot books are white, the inclusion of Black illustrators represents a significant step forward in the world of children's books.

Since many of the melting pot stories are satisfying but slight, one might expect them to be out of print in a relatively short period. However, the quality of the illustrations, along with their timeliness, has probably contributed to their longevity. Only a few of the melting pot books have been published since 1975, but almost all of them were still listed in the 1979-1980 *Books in Print*.

Conclusion

The melting pot books represent a major improvement over invisibility and over most of the social conscience books. For the most part, they transcend the demeaning images of the past and provide in their place positive images of Afro-American children and their families. They avoid such grim social problems as poverty, drugs, and gangs, which are part of some of the "Black experience" books for older children. As a group, they create that imaginary, racially integrated social order in which the grandchildren of former slaves and the white grandchildren of former slaveholders do live and work together harmoniously, and in which the grandchildren of slaves have assimilated and have been assimilated into the larger white cultural milieu. Within that milieu, the personal problems and experiences shared are those of other American children—sibling relationships, growing pains, and so forth.

On one level, to project such a social order is a positive act. It permits one to assume a primary audience of both Black and white readers, since presumably any American child can find himself or herself and his or her life experiences mirrored in such books. It also allows for the integration of the all-white world of children's books.

Obviously, such books do not require any consciousness or sensibility or perspective that might be labeled Afro-American, since it is precisely that perspective that is omitted from the melting pot books, presumably by choice. Ray Anthony Shepard (1971), in a controversial article in the *Interracial Books for Children Bulletin*, compares Ezra Jack Keats's books unfavorably to those of John Steptoe, a young Black artist. Shepard asserts that Keats creates kids who only *look* Black, while Steptoe's kids "know what's happening." The point is that the melting pot books intend to do just that—create kids who are Afro-American in appearance only, who reflect only the non-Afro side of the Afro-American duality, and because that is their intention, they are successful to the extent that the literary and artistic qualities of the books hold up.

On some other level, however, one must ask at what point the ignoring of differences becomes a signal that the recognition of them makes people uncomfortable or unhappy. Physical descriptions are frequently given in the text of books as part of character delineation. When they are deliberately and systematically avoided in books featuring Blacks, the differences begin to lose their neutrality; the implication is that unlike physical, linguistic, and sociocultural differences among Euro-Americans, differences between Euro-Americans and Afro-Americans signify something undesirable. To ignore linguistic and sociocultural characteristics of a large group of children may be another means of conferring a kind of invisibility on them. They are permitted to exist in books only so long as they conform to the norm of middle-class Euro-American social and cultural values and life experiences.

As has been pointed out, one must recognize the existence and validity of an Afro-American middle-class experience, as well as the need to reflect that experience in Afro-American literature. But as a group, the melting pot books, in their portrayal of Afro-American experience, seem not only to hide the smoke of cultural differences, but to extinguish the fire of cultural distinctness. Killens (1971) asserts that "a story that could have been about anybody is probably a story that could have been about precisely nobody at all" (p. 381).

If the body of children's realistic fiction about Afro-Americans consisted solely of social conscience and melting pot books, it would be inadequate to meet the demands of those who wish to see the world of children's books integrated. What would be missing would be literature that recognizes the existence of Afro-American experiences, tries to reflect its truths, celebrates its distinctness, and at the same time affirms the universality of all human experience.

The Melting Pot Books

Afro-Americans in Stories about Non-Afro-Americans

Alexander, Martha. *Sabrina*. New York: Dial Press, 1971. (Preschool–Gr. 2)*

Caudill, Rebecca. *A Certain Small Shepherd*. New York: Holt, Rinehart and Winston, 1965. (Gr. K–6)

Clymer, Eleanor. *Luke Was There*. Illus. by Diane DeGroat. New York: Holt, Rinehart and Winston, 1973. (Gr. 3–5)

Durham, John. *Me and Arch and the Pest*. Illus. by Ingrid Fetz. New York: Four Winds Press, 1970. (Gr. 3–5) O.P.**

Hoffman, Phyllis. *Steffie and Me*. Illus. by Emily Arnold McCully. New York: Harper and Row, 1970. (Gr. 1–4)

Konigsburg, E. L. *Jennifer, Hecate, MacBeth, William McKinley and Me, Elizabeth*. New York: Atheneum, 1967. (Gr. 3–8)

Merrill, Jean. *The Toothpaste Millionaire*. Boston: Houghton Mifflin, 1972. (Gr. 2–5)

---

*Grade level designations from the 1979–1980 *Books in Print*.
**O.P. = Out of Print.

Afro-American Children in Integrated Settings

Alexander, Martha. *Bobo's Dream.* New York: Dial Press, 1970. (Preschool-Gr. 2)

Breinburg, Petronella. *Shawn Goes to School.* Illus. by Erroll Lloyd. New York: Thomas Y. Crowell, 1973. (Preschool-Gr. 2)

Burchardt, Nellie. *Project Cat.* Illus. by Fermin Rocker. New York: Franklin Watts, 1966. (Gr. 2-4) O.P.

Desbarats, Peter. *Gabrielle and Selena.* Illus. by Nancy Grossman. New York: Harcourt, Brace, and World, 1968. (Gr. K-3)

Glasser, Barbara. *Leroy, OOPS.* Illus. by Lee Jack Morton. Chicago: Cowles Book Corp., 1971. (Gr. 1-5)

Grifalconi, Ann. *City Rhythms.* Indianapolis: Bobbs-Merrill, 1965. (Gr. K-3)

Horvath, Betty. *Hooray for Jasper.* Illus. by Fermin Rocker. New York: Franklin Watts, 1966. (Gr. K-2) O.P.

Isadora, Rachel. *Willaby.* New York: Macmillan, 1977. (Gr. K-2)

Kempner, Carol. *Nicholas.* New York: Simon and Schuster, 1968. (Preschool-Gr. 3)

Klimowicz, Barbara. *When Shoes Eat Socks.* Illus. by Gloria Kamen. Nashville: Abingdon Press, 1971. (Gr. K-2)

Lovelace, Maud. *The Valentine Box.* Illus. by Ingrid Fetz. New York: Thomas Y. Crowell, 1966. (Gr. K-4)

Weil, Lisl. *Fat Ernest.* New York: Parents Magazine Press, 1973. (Gr. K-3)

Black Children, Black Families

Burch, Robert. *Joey's Cat.* Illus. by Don Freeman. New York: Viking Press, 1969. (Preschool-Gr. 2)

Caines, Jeannette. *Abby.* Illus. by Steven Kellogg. New York: Harper and Row, 1973. (Preschool-Gr. 3)

Caines, Jeannette. *Daddy.* Illus. by Ronald Himler. New York: Harper and Row, 1977. (Gr. K-3)

Clifton, Lucille. *Don't You Remember?* Illus. by Evaline Ness. New York: E. P. Dutton, 1973. (Preschool-Gr. 2)

Hill, Elizabeth Starr. *Evan's Corner.* Illus. by Nancy Grossman. New York: Holt, Rinehart and Winston, 1967. (Gr. K-3)

Jensen, Virginia A. *Sara and the Door.* Illus. by Ann Strugnell. Reading, Mass.: Addison-Wesley, 1977. (Gr. K-1)

Keats, Ezra Jack. *The Snowy Day.* New York: Viking Press, 1962. (Gr. K-3)

Keats, Ezra Jack. *Whistle for Willie.* New York: Viking Press, 1964. (Gr. K-3)

Keats, Ezra Jack. *Peter's Chair.* New York: Harper and Row, 1967. (Gr. K-3)

Keats, Ezra Jack. *A Letter to Amy.* New York: Harper and Row, 1968. (Gr. K-2) O.P.

Keats, Ezra Jack. *Goggles!* New York: Macmillan, 1969. (Gr. K-2)

Keats, Ezra Jack. *Hi, Cat!* New York: Macmillan, 1970. (Gr. K-3)

Keats, Ezra Jack. *Pet Show!* New York: Macmillan, 1972. (Gr. K-3)

Lexau, Joan. *Me Day.* Illus. by Robert Weaver. New York: Dial Press, 1971. (Preschool-Gr. 3)

Miles, Miska. *Mississippi Possum*. Illus. by John Schoenherr. Boston: Little, Brown and Co., 1965. (Gr. 2-6)

Palmer, Candida. *A Ride on High*. Illus. by H. Tom Hall. New York: J. B. Lippincott, 1966. (Gr. K-3)

Prather, Ray. *No Trespassing*. New York: Macmillan, 1974. (Gr. K-3)

Rosenblatt, Suzanne. *Everyone Is Going Somewhere*. New York: Macmillan, 1976. (Gr. K-2)

Scott, Ann Herbert. *Big Cowboy Western*. Illus. by Richard W. Lewis. New York: Lothrop, Lee and Shepard, 1965. (Gr. K-3)

Scott, Ann Herbert. *Sam*. Illus. by Symeon Shimin. New York: McGraw-Hill, 1967. (Preschool-Gr. 3)

Sharmat, Marjorie. *I Don't Care*. Illus. by Lillian Hoban. New York: Macmillan, 1977. (Preschool-Gr. 1)

Thomas, Ianthe. *Eliza's Daddy*. Illus. by Moneta Barnett. New York: Harcourt Brace Jovanovich, 1976. (Gr. 1-5)

Udry, Janice M. *What Mary Jo Shared*. Chicago: Alfred Whitman and Co., 1966. (Gr. K-2)

4 Culturally Conscious Fiction: Reflections of Afro-American Experience

My soul look back and wonder
How I got over

Gospel Song by Clara Ward

Appearing throughout the period of this survey, 1965 to 1979, but dominating from the middle seventies on, is a third group of books about Afro-Americans. These books come closest to constituting a body of Afro-American literature for children. They are books that reflect, with varying degrees of success, the social and cultural traditions associated with growing up Black in the United States. In contrast to the social conscience books, they are not primarily addressed to non-Blacks, nor are they focused on desegregating neighborhoods or schools. They differ from the melting pot books in that they recognize, sometimes even celebrate, the distinctiveness of the experience of growing up simultaneously Black and American. Their primary intent is to speak to Afro-American children about themselves and their lives, though as has been pointed out, they are by no means closed to other children. These books must be considered an important component of American children's literature in general.

The label *culturally conscious* suggests that elements in the text, not just the pictures, make it clear that the book consciously seeks to depict a fictional Afro-American life experience. At minimum this means that the major characters are Afro-Americans, the story is told from their perspective, the setting is an Afro-American community or home, and the text includes some means of identifying the characters as Black—physical descriptions, language, cultural traditions, and so forth.

The general aim of the culturally conscious books is presumably to help Black children understand "how we got over." In a chapter entitled "How I Got Ovuh," Smitherman (1977) explains that "gittin ovuh" is about survival, both in a spiritual and a material sense. Her book, *Talkin and Testifyin*, is a description of the language of Black Americans, and in this chapter Smitherman argues:

> In Black America, the oral tradition has served as a fundamental
> vehicle for gittin ovuh. That tradition preserves the Afro-Ameri-
> can heritage and reflects the collective spirit of the race. Through
> song, story, folk sayings, and rich verbal interplay among every-
> day people, lessons and precepts about life and survival are
> handed down from generation to generation. [P. 73]

Reflections of this oral tradition are among the most distinctive
features of culturally conscious realistic fiction about Afro-Americans. It is mirrored not only in the dialogue between and among
characters, but often in the narration itself, as a part of the
author's style. An awareness of this tradition manifests itself, too,
in an author's inclusion of settings and situations in which certain
rhetorical styles naturally occur, such as church services or gather-
ings of teenaged boys.

Culturally conscious books also reflect other cultural behaviors,
institutions, and traditions that are part of Afro-American life
experiences. Smitherman suggests that Black communication systems are grounded in a traditional African world view—"an underlying set of thought patterns, belief sets, values, ways of looking at
the world" (p. 74). Citing African and other scholars, she asserts
that while the manifestations of this world view are diverse and
complex and have not survived in their totality for Afro-Americans, it is nevertheless appropriate to speak of a traditional African
world view as an entity, and to recognize its residue in the life-
styles and world views of Afro-Americans. This world view not
only underlies Black communications systems but is part of what
was referred to in the first chapter as an Afro-American sensibility.
Thus, such diverse elements as traditional Black church services,
references to voodoo, especially close relationships between the
young and the old, extended families, child-rearing practices,
respect for elders, and the belief in the gift of second sight may be
rooted in a traditional African world view. This view emphasizes
(1) the harmony between things spiritual and material, (2) the
hierarchical nature and cyclical rhythm of the universe, and (3) the
harmony of opposites—the idea that "opposites" such as the
spiritual and the material are interdependent forces, both of which
are necessary to existence (pp. 74–76). The inclusion of such elements in many of the culturally conscious books is another characteristic that sets these books apart from the other two groups,
and indicates the extent to which the author is sensitive to those
aspects of Afro-American life and is capable of reflecting them,
or willing to do so, in the fictional world being created.

The culturally conscious books are also distinguishable, in some cases, by their general theme or topic or by their treatment of the theme. One such general theme is oppression. Books centered on the oppression theme usually present Afro-Americans trying to achieve some goal in the face of overt racism and discrimination. Closely related to the oppression theme is that of survival, sometimes in the physical sense, sometimes in the sense of merely maintaining one's sense of dignity in the face of oppression. The tragic-mulatto theme, which was common in the literature of the Harlem Renaissance, presents the phenomenon of trying to cope with the status of having been born of mixed racial parentage and not feeling accepted as either Black or white. The tragic mulatto is not prevalent in contemporary children's fiction but does appear in at least one book, *With My Face to the Rising Sun* (Screen, 1977). More common in children's fiction is the idea of finding oneself, which is also prevalent in general realistic fiction for children. In books about Afro-Americans, this theme often relates to coming to grips with one's sense of what it means to be Afro-American, as in Louretta Hawkin's exploration of the concept of "soul" in *The Soul Brothers and Sister Lou* (Hunter, 1968).

The previous themes and linguistic and cultural traditions are reflected throughout many of the culturally conscious books. However, for discussion purposes, the eighty-nine culturally conscious books in the survey have been divided into seven groups: (1) African and "Down Home" Heritage and Traditions, (2) Common Everyday Experiences, (3) Surviving Racism and Discrimination, (4) Living in the City, (5) Friendships and Peer Relationships, (6) Family Relationships, and (7) Growing Up and Finding Oneself. The discussion is divided into two major parts: a description of the types of books included in the category and an analysis of the content of the books.

African and "Down Home" Heritage and Traditions

Since this survey is concerned with contemporary realistic fiction, several important types of books about Afro-Americans have been excluded: historical fiction, nonfiction/information books, and books about African experiences and traditions. However, several books of realistic fiction, all picture books with one exception, focus on either an African heritage, an Afro-American heritage, or "down home" traditions, that is, southern rural traditions, within the context of a contemporary United States setting.

Three such books focus on African heritage and traditions. Lucille Clifton's *All Us Come Cross the Water* (1973) and John Steptoe's *Birthday* (1972), both illustrated by Steptoe, are rather self-conscious affirmations of Afro-American unity—"We one people, Ujamaa. . . . All us crossed the water"—and the concept of "nation time." *Birthday* relates the celebration of Javaka's eighth birthday in Yoruba, an imaginary Afro-American commune. *Cornrows* (Yarbrough, 1979) shows a modern family celebrating the richness of the traditional African custom of plaiting one's hair in what southern Blacks came to call cornrows.

Virginia Hamilton's *The House of Dies Drear* (1968), the one nonpicture book in this group, and Lucille Clifton's *The Lucky Stone* (1979) both incorporate some historical information from the slave period. Dies Drear's house is in Ohio and at one time had been a station on the Underground Railroad. It is purchased by a Black historian, whose family becomes involved in unearthing alleged ghosts and solving the mystery of the house of Dies Drear. In the process, the children acquire a considerable amount of Afro-American history, which is skillfully woven into the texture of the story. *The Lucky Stone* is passed down through four generations of Black women, each of whom has found the stone to be lucky for her. The first owner had been a runaway slave, who used it to let other slaves know where she was hiding. They, in turn, secretly fed her until it was safe for her to reappear, after Emancipation.

Four other books focus on traditional southern rural experiences. The controversial *Oh Lord, I Wish I Was a Buzzard* (Greenberg, 1968) relates the experience of picking cotton "when I was a little girl" on a day when it was so hot and picking such unpleasant work that the narrator wishes she could be every animal that she sees, including a buzzard. *Lordy, Aunt Hattie* (Thomas, 1973) and *Raccoons Are for Loving* (Bourne, 1968) both feature dialogue between an older woman and a young girl about southern rural experiences, though *Raccoons Are for Loving* is set in an urban area. *Mr. Kelso's Lion* (Bontemps, 1970) relates Percy's adventures when he and his grandfather visit Aunt Clothilde in Sidonia, Alabama.

As a group, this set of books abounds with the language and lore of Afro-Americans. Clearly, these books were intended to put Afro-American children in touch with their history, at least in a spiritual sense. That is, they are not historical fiction as such, but seem designed to permit today's Afro-American children to reach out to their past and to find their connections to it.

Probably the most striking characteristic of these books, as a group, is the richness of their language. Some, such as *Lordy, Aunt Hattie* and *Oh Lord, I Wish I Was a Buzzard*, are poetic in their use of rhythm and imagery. *Cornrows* excels in this regard, weaving rhythm and rhyme into a family's weaving of hair into cornrows. In addition, the books by Clifton, Thomas, and Bontemps demonstrate that those authors' ears were acutely tuned to the everyday vernacular of southern Blacks, while Steptoe and Clifton were equally adept at capturing modern urban Black vernacular. Bontemps, in *Mr. Kelso's Lion*, also incorporates some elements of Afro-American folk literature, such as the Blacks-can't-win relationship between Blacks and whites and some humor at the expense of Black preachers.

It is interesting to note that the one controversial book in this subset focuses on the experience of picking cotton. *Oh Lord, I Wish I Was a Buzzard* is based on the experiences of a Black woman and has much to recommend it—repetitive, rhythmical, lyrical language, and illustrations that capture the beauty of the land. However, the book appeared in 1968, a time when the plantation imagery it evoked and its unfortunate references to a Black child's wishing to be such animals as a snake and a buzzard were unwelcome contrasts to the then-current emphasis on the more positive and lesser-known aspects of Afro-American history and culture.

Common Everyday Experiences

Included in the survey is a set of seven picture books that, much like Keats's *The Snowy Day*, present vignettes of everyday experiences of Afro-American children. Unlike Peter in *The Snowy Day*, however, the main characters in these books have not been culturally homogenized.

Two of these books, *Fly, Jimmy, Fly* (Myers, 1974) and *I Been There* (Calloway, 1977), present young Afro-American boys in urban settings using their imaginations to create adventures for themselves. Jimmy watches the birds and thinks he should be able to fly. "You ain't no bird," his mama said. But he discovered that his imagination could set him free, even if lifting his own brown arms and jumping off an orange crate only resulted in an injured knee. The unnamed narrator in *I Been There*, in a much more con-

trived and less effective book, goes up to the rooftop and day-
dreams about a trip to outer space, where he uses an African spear
to fight off a challenge from a nineteen-foot gorilla bat.

The journey in the third of these picture books is real enough.
Flip in *Downtown Is* (Thomas, 1972) lives around 125th Street
and St. Nicholas Avenue and does not know downtown Manhattan
at all. The book describes his visit to mid-Manhattan. *Uptown*
(Steptoe, 1970), on the other hand, describes the uptown Harlem
environment of two boys who envision the lives of the people they
see—junkies, cops, Brothers, hippies.

Stevie (Steptoe, 1969) was probably the most successful of these
picture books. Published when Steptoe was just nineteen, it describes, in Black English, Robert's reminiscences of Stevie, the
little boy who used to stay with Robert's family while his own
mother worked. *First Pink Light* (Greenfield, 1976) tells what hap-
pens when Tyree tries to stay up all night (till the first pink light
of dawn) to wait for his father's return from a trip.

Hi, Mrs. Mallory! (Thomas, 1979) has been included here,
although there may be as strong an argument for calling it a melting pot book. It describes the warm and very special relationship
between a Black girl and an elderly white woman. The setting is
the rural South, which is reflected in the language and experience
described. There is no text reference to Li'l Bits being Black, and
it is difficult to identify her language as different from Mrs.
Mallory's. On the other hand, these are most certainly not culturally homogenized characters and seem clearly distinguishable from
the melting-pot book characters, probably because of the regional
flavor of the text.

On one level, all of these books are similar to the melting pot
books in the sense that the experiences presented are, for the most
part, those that may well have happened to Any Child. The fact
of being an Afro-American does not play an important role in any
of the books (except to the extent that it plays a role in living in
Harlem). On the other hand, all of these books, set in an Afro-
American cultural milieu, reflect some aspect of that culture,
although there is some variation in the degree to which the books
can be called Afro-American. The language of *First Pink Light* is
standard English, and there is just one reference to the "strong
brown face" of Tyree's father. *Stevie, Uptown,* and *Fly, Jimmy,
Fly* are, by contrast, full of Black English vernacular, and *Fly,
Jimmy, Fly* also includes references to skin color and "soul food"—
collard greens and fat back. *Downtown Is* simply plants its major

character on the streets of Harlem. The apparent point of these books is to present in an unself-conscious manner Afro-American children going about the business of everyday living.

Surviving Racism and Discrimination

These books, along with some of the "living in the city" books, are in one sense the other side of the coin from the social conscience fiction. A major part of the focus is on conflicts between Blacks and whites, but in contrast with the social conscience fiction, the conflict is viewed from the perspective of the Afro-Americans. A further contrast to the social conscience fiction is the lack of focus on racial integration as a goal of Afro-Americans. The goal of the characters in these books is to achieve their own ends—such as survival, landholding, education, a sense of independence—in the face of racism, discrimination, violence, and other misuses of white economic and political power.

Surprisingly few in number (five in this survey), these books were preceded by older "achieving-against-the-odds" books, such as Jesse Jackson's *Call Me Charley* (New York: Harper and Row, 1945), and Hope Newell's *A Cap for Mary Ellis* (New York: Harper and Row, 1952). This group might also be larger if it included the entire set of Lorenz Graham's "town" books—*South Town* (Chicago: Follett, 1958), *North Town* (New York: T. Y. Crowell, 1965), *Whose Town?* (1969), and *Return to South Town* (New York: T. Y. Crowell, 1976)—which follow David Williams and his family from David's adolescence through his return to his hometown to set up medical practice. Only one representative title of that set, *Whose Town?*, is included. However, this group does include both of Mildred Taylor's books about the Logan family. *Roll of Thunder, Hear My Cry* (1976), which won the Newbery Medal, is an expansion and extension of the first, *Song of the Trees* (1975).

Included in this group, too, is the one book in the survey that develops the tragic-mulatto theme, the previously mentioned book by Screen, *With My Face to the Rising Sun*. In the opening scene, a young Black boy is killed by some white golfers over a stray golf ball. His two Black friends, Richard and Ben, escape with their lives. The book then relates the story of Richard's search for identity in the face of several complex circumstances, including his grandfather's refusal to let him testify in the death of his friend, his subsequent rejection by the other Black children, his grandfather's rejection of him and all dark-skinned Blacks, and his traumatic discovery that his own father was white. Unlike the other books in this category, this autobiographical novel is unrelievedly grim and seems more like a personal psychological exploration than a book meant to touch the lives of young readers.

As a group, these books tend to celebrate the courage and determination of Afro-American families and individuals who are faced with racism, oppression, or violence. Their responses range from riots to boycotts, to use of the legal system, to desperate last-ditch individual stands. *Whose Town?* and *Sneakers* (Shepard, 1973), both set in northern cities, affirm the idea that while Blacks must take responsibility for their own lives, Blacks and whites can learn to coexist—that people must be judged as individuals. *Whose Town?* suggests that many of "the Negro's" problems could be solved by education, hard work, and right living and, further, that the struggle is not Black against white, but people against evil and hate. Still, the focus is not on being accepted in a white cultural milieu. *Song of the Trees* and *Roll of Thunder, Hear My Cry*, set in Mississippi during an earlier period, are less optimistic in regard to Black/white coexistence. David Logan, in *Song of the Trees*, seems to sum up the position of these books: "A Black man's always gotta be ready to die. And it don't make me any difference if I die today or tomorrow. Just so long as I die right. . . . It don't matter none. 'Cause I'll always have my self respect."

Living in the City

The second largest subset of culturally conscious books, numbering twenty titles, focuses on urban living. While many books about Afro-Americans are set in cities, in these books the city seems almost to take on a life of its own and to impose its own conditions on the lives of the human characters. Unfortunately, the picture of city life is mainly sad and grim—defined by gangs, drugs, poverty, violence, and crime.

With two exceptions, all the books in this category that were published in the late sixties were written by non-Black authors: *Durango Street* (Bonham, 1965), *The Jazz Man* (Weik, 1966), *The Contender* (Lipsyte, 1967), *How Many Miles to Babylon* (Fox, 1967), *Member of the Gang* (Rinkoff, 1968), *Behind the Magic Line* (Erwin, 1969). The two books written by Black authors were *Harlem Summer* (Vroman, 1967) and the previously mentioned book by Hunter, *The Soul Brothers and Sister Lou*. All except *The Soul Brothers and Sister Lou* and *Behind the Magic Line* feature males as the major characters. Not until the seventies is a move to Black authors and female heroes prevalent.

Several of the city books present young men resisting the pressure to become members of street gangs or to aid gang activities. Not one of these books was written by a Black author. In two cases, *How Many Miles to Babylon* and *Trouble on Treat Street* (Alexander, 1974), young boys are accosted by other boys who have formed gangs. *Trouble on Treat Street* casts a young Black boy, Clem, with his neighbor Manolo, a Chicano. They both are assaulted by a gang of older boys and learn to be friends, as do their very religious grandmother and mother, in spite of the clash of cultures and oppressive environment they face. In *How Many Miles to Babylon*, a much more sensitive book by a highly skilled writer, James is kidnapped by a group of boys who want to use him in their racket of stealing dogs and returning them for reward money.

Rufus, of *Durango Street*, and Woodie, of *Member of the Gang*, both become members of gangs; each, by the end of the book, appears to be headed for reform—with the aid of understanding male social workers. Both these books read as if they might have been written by the social workers, although *Durango Street* also shows the touch of a professional writer.

In *The Contender*, Alfred Brooks uses boxing to find himself and to help decide what to do with his life. His experiences with a gang are peripheral, since he refuses to join the group and is concerned only because his friend James is a part of a gang.

The boys in these books are generally fatherless and poor, and are often truants living in dark ghettos. The point seems to be to "tell it like it is," to alert readers to the stark realities of ghetto living, perhaps to arouse sympathy. That they manage to end on hopeful notes belies the relentless grimness with which most of the lives of the characters are depicted.

Harlem Summer was the first of the books in this survey to "tell it like it is" from the perspective of an Afro-American author. It is the skillfully written story of sixteen-year-old John Brown's experiences in Harlem when he arrives from Montgomery, Alabama, to spend the summer with his aunt and uncle. Although John, too, meets with crime, violence, and harshness in the city, he also has high aspirations, serious heroes, and a sense of his ties to other Blacks who have struggled for civil rights.

The Soul Brothers and Sister Lou, however, is probably considered the "breakthrough" book of this category, perhaps because its hero is a fourteen-year-old girl; her age makes the book the first of its kind written by a Black author for younger readers. It also was the first winner of the minority writers contest of the Council on Interracial Books for Children and was thereby well publicized. Full of the details of everyday life of Blacks living in a large city ghetto, it is also full of some of the cruel realities of that life—lack of money, lack of adequate housing, lack of recreational facilities for youth, violence, police hostility, and so forth. In the midst of this harshness, Louretta is searching for her own sense of self, for the meaning of "soul."

Two of the city books focus on the devastating effect of drugs on young people and their families. Alice Childress's *A Hero Ain't Nothin' but a Sandwich* (1974) tells the story of thirteen-year-old Benjie and the people who try to save him from his drug habit. Sharon Bell Mathis's *Teacup Full of Roses* (1972) presents a young man trying to hold on to his own dreams and those of his younger brother in the face of his father's weakness and his mother's blind refusal to deal with anyone but her oldest son, who is already lost to drugs.

The urban grimness also appears in *na-ni* (Deveaux, 1973), in which a welfare check is stolen; in *His Own Where* (Jordan, 1971), in which a young couple must find a way to survive almost solely on love; and in *It Ain't All for Nothin'* (Myers, 1978), in which a boy must ultimately choose to free himself by turning in his own father, who has been involved in an armed robbery and who seems unable to save either himself or his son. *The Jazz Man* was an earlier harbinger of such books. In it a lame and hungry child is apparently abandoned temporarily by his parents.

A few of the city books are less grim, and while the city or city living still imposes itself on the stories and the characters' lives, its influence seems less oppressive. In *Sidewalk Story* (Mathis, 1971), for example, Lilly Etta's determination makes a difference when her best friend Tanya's family is evicted and their furniture placed on the sidewalk. *Willy* (King, 1971) is about a rat who is trapped and destroyed by a young boy who feels it his responsibility to be "the man of the family." *Little Man, Little Man* (1977), James Baldwin's venture into the juvenile market, presents everyday experiences of T.J., a five-year-old growing up in Harlem, where life is hard and conditions are sometimes hazardous, but sometimes fun. *Maple Street* (Agle, 1970) is somewhat like the social conscience books in that Margaret works through the system to have a vacant lot turned into a park and her family befriends a hostile poor white family who moves in next door.

Walter Dean Myers has produced several books set in the city. Like many of the less grim, more optimistic, and more positive portrayals of city life, *The Dancers* (1972) is a book for younger children. It is a picture book in which Michael gets to meet ballet dancers who are rehearsing at the theatre where his father works. They, in turn, visit Michael and his friends in their neighborhood. Each group learns something of the other's way of dancing. Myers's *The Young Landlords* (1979) involves a group of teenagers who buy a tenement for $1.00 and then face, with humor and ingenuity, the problem of how to be responsible landlords.

With a few exceptions, the picture of city life that emerges from these books is depressing. While in most cases the protagonists emerge hopeful and whole, their experiences have been grim indeed. More than one has been beaten, abandoned by parents, poisoned by drugs. They have participated, reluctantly or willingly, in criminal activities. A few witnessed the violent deaths of friends or loved ones. At least half of the households in these books are fatherless. But in spite of the conditions depicted, a few books emphasize the strengths and resources available within the individual and the support from family and friends that can enable people to cope.

Friendships and Peer Relationships

Another group of culturally conscious books, generally also set in the city, focuses on developing friendships, or close relationships, with people outside the immediate family. If there is a general theme, it is that even though maintaining a friendship entails considerable commitment and responsibility, friends are to be valued as a very important part of our lives.

Two picture books are included in this group. In *Three Wishes* (Clifton, 1974), Zenobia temporarily loses and then regains the valued friendship of her neighbor, Victorius. *The Soul of Christmas* (King, 1972) presents the idea that Christmas is about giving and helping others.

Among the nonpicture books dealing with friendship is Clifton's *The Times They Used to Be* (1974), which tells, in flashback, of the friendship between two young girls, Tassie and Sookie. *Who Goes There, Lincoln?* (Fife, 1975) is one of a series of slight, mediocre books about Lincoln Barnum. This story tells of Lincoln and his friends' efforts to find a new clubhouse and initiate some new members. As it turns out, their chosen site had been a station on the Underground Railroad. *That Ruby* (Brown, 1969) is a rather contrived and patronizing story in which Ruby, who is poor, tough, belligerent, but vulnerable, is befriended by more privileged classmates. Hamilton's *The Planet of Junior Brown* (1971) is a complex tale of the friendship between Junior, a huge musical prodigy; Buddy, a street kid on his own; and Mr. Poole, an ex-teacher and current janitor in a junior high school. *The Friends* (Guy, 1973) concerns a friendship between Edith, a poor, feisty "ragamuffin," and Phylissia, whose overprotective West Indian father does not want her to associate with someone like Edith.

Two of the Walter Dean Myers stories have been placed here also: *Fast Sam, Cool Clyde, and Stuff* (1975) and *Mojo and the Russians* (1977). Both present, with much warmth and humor, groups of adolescents growing up in New York City. The South is the setting for *William* (Hunt, 1977), which involves a friendship that turns into a family relationship among William, his two sisters, and Sarah, a white, unmarried teenage mother.

The friendship books are much like other realistic fiction centering on the same topic. What places these in a "culturally conscious" category is that they are full of the details of everyday living in Black families and communities. They are distinguished by their use of Black English, by references to such traditional lore as the possession of second sight, and the belief that "when a good man be the first person in your house on New Year's Day," you will have good luck all year.

Family Relationships

Another set of the culturally conscious books focuses on relationships within a family unit. Some concentrate on relationships among the children. *My Brother Fine with Me* (Clifton, 1975) and *She Come Bringing Me That Little Baby Girl* (Greenfield, 1974) feature older siblings who are at first resentful of a younger brother or sister and then realize their love for the child. In *New Life, New Room* (Jordan, 1975), a family works out a way to make room for a new baby in an already overcrowded apartment. When James Edward needs someone to share his good news in Greenfield's book *Good News* (1972), he settles on his baby sister. *Anthony and Sabrina* (Prather, 1973) and *Timothy, the Terror* (Cavin, 1972) present the activities of brothers and sisters playing together.

Other books focus on families who plan or play together as a unit. *Striped Ice Cream* (Lexau, 1968) tells of the birthday surprise Betsy's family plans for her. *Boss Cat* (Hunter, 1971) is the humorous story of a Black family's adoption by a cat, over the strong objections of the mother. *Amifika* (Clifton, 1977) learns that he is not about to be thrown out to make room for his father, who is returning from military service. One very special book, *The Hundred Penny Box* (Mathis, 1975), describes the relationship between Michael and his one-hundred-year-old Aunt Dewbet Thomas.

The family books for older children tend to focus on young people concerned about conflicts within the family unit, often between the adults, as in Greenfield's *Talk about a Family* (1978) and Ernest Gaines's *A Long Day in November* (1971). In *Sister* (Greenfield, 1974), Doretha copes with her sister's withdrawal and hostility after the death of their father. In *Nobody's Family Is Going to Change* (Fitzhugh, 1974), Emma learns that lesson about her family. Overweight, she wants to be a lawyer, an ambition that her parents find laughable. Her brother wants to be a dancer, and that choice is totally unacceptable to their father.

Like the books that focus on friendship, the culturally conscious books that focus on family relationships are distinguishable mainly by their perspective on life and on the details of everyday living that are included: Black vernacular, terms of address, family nicknames. The families are, for the most part, intact nuclear families. Only three have missing fathers, and the death of one father is central to the story itself. Only one family includes three generations living together, although grandparents appear in two others.

Growing Up and Finding Oneself

The largest group of culturally conscious books, including twenty-four titles, focuses on youngsters making some step(s) toward maturity as individuals. While the protagonists often are also involved in relationships with family and peers, the stories involve (1) achieving some personal goal, (2) acquiring some insight into themselves as individuals, (3) recognizing their growth over a given period of time, or, especially in the case of the books for older readers, (4) some combination of the above.

The simplest of these books are the ones that focus on achieving some goal. They are often picture books and, in this survey, are generally about boys. The boys' achievements vary from earning enough money to buy a guitar (*Song of the Empty Bottles,*

Molarsky, 1968) to finding a quiet place (*A Quiet Place*, Blue, 1969), to finding spring (*The Boy Who Didn't Believe in Spring*, Clifton, 1973), to going to the store alone (*I Can Do It by Myself*, Little and Greenfield, 1978). Two books, *Scat!* (Dobrin, 1971) and *Ben's Trumpet* (Isadora, 1979), involve boys who yearn and learn to play jazz music.

Several books center on young people's achieving some insight into themselves, or "finding" themselves, in a sense. Interestingly, these books tend to have girls as their major characters. In *Zeely* (Hamilton, 1967), Elizabeth learns in her interaction with Zeely that it is important to be oneself and to hold on to one's own way of seeing the world. *Tessie* (Jackson, 1968) learns that she can keep one foot in Hobbe, a mostly white private school, and the other at home in Harlem. "Hobbe is third base, the block is home." Beth, in *Philip Hall Likes Me, I Reckon, Maybe* (Greene, 1974), learns that she does not have to hold back in second place in order to be friends with "cute" Philip Hall. *Nellie Cameron* (Murray, 1971), who considers herself a failure at reading, learns that she is loved, that she can learn to read, and that she must learn to define herself in her own terms.

Other books focus on growing, on a character's recognition that he or she has moved a step or two closer to maturity. In Nikki Grimes's story *Growin'* (1977), Yolanda (Pumpkin) grows into the realization that "when hard times come, good feeling people stick together." *Ludell* (Wilkinson, 1975) and *Ludell and Willie* (Wilkinson, 1977) chronicle some of the experiences of growing up that a young girl has while living in Waycross, Georgia, with her strict grandmother.

Not unexpectedly, the most complex books in the group combine elements of achieving goals, gaining insights into oneself, and growing toward maturity. While some such books feature relatively more mature or older protagonists—Willie Carver in *Fast Break Forward* (Etter, 1969) or Edith Jackson in Rosa Guy's book (1978) of that title—others, such as Hamilton's *Arilla Sun Down* (1976) and *M.C. Higgins, the Great* (1974), develop complex themes in greater depth and on more than one level.

As with the family and friendships books, the distinctiveness of the growing-up books lies, in general, in the authenticating details—the language, the typical activities, the values of the characters, their attitudes, and so forth. Several are also distinct in that the main characters are trying to come to grips with their racial and cultural identity.

Analyzing the Culturally Conscious Books

This survey of fiction about Afro-Americans has three underlying concerns: (1) presumed primary audience, (2) the recognition and characterization of a distinct Afro-American experience, and (3) the perspective from which the books appear to have been written. In the case of the culturally conscious books, the assertion has been that their primary audience is presumed to be Afro-American children. It has also been asserted that by definition these books consciously seek to reflect distinctly Afro-American life experiences. The following analysis attempts to confirm those assertions and to examine further the two remaining aspects of those issues—the differing perspectives from which they appear to have been written and the characterizing of Afro-American experiences in these books.

Perspective

From what perspective have realistic books about Afro-American experiences been written? In the case of the social conscience books, it seems clear that they were written, as George Woods suggested, by white authors for white children. The point where those authors stood to view the world about which they wrote was clearly outside any Afro-American cultural milieu. In the case of the melting pot books, the author either again stood outside an Afro-American setting or stepped inside a circumscribed portion of it—that portion that overlaps and coalesces with majority white cultural traditions and values. It is the culturally conscious books, then, that purportedly depict distinctly Afro-American experiences and that are most influenced by the author's perspective on those experiences.

While the issue is often discussed in terms of whether white authors can write about Afro-American experiences, it has been argued earlier that the issue is racially related only to the extent that a sensitivity to Afro-American cultural and linguistic traditions is racially related to Afro-American sensibilities and world view. White authors can create books of merit about Afro-Americans, as has been seen with the melting pot books. Usually, however, culturally conscious books by white authors differ in subtle or sometimes glaring ways from the same kind of books by Afro-American authors. The differences seem to have at least two dimensions—emphasis and authenticating detail.

Not surprisingly, those differences are least apparent and on some level least significant in modern picture books. Therefore, as in the melting pot books, some of the best of the culturally conscious books by white authors are the picture books. The brevity of the books and the fact that the pictures are an integral part of the story itself release the author from the need to include much detail at all. The age level for which most picture books are intended precludes an emphasis on some of the sordid reality found in books for older children. Thus, the author of a picture book can create a good culturally conscious book, as defined in this survey, by the use of setting, by the creation of an ambience, and, of course, by telling a good story and telling it well. *Sunflowers for Tina* (Baldwin, 1970), *Song of the Empty Bottles*, and *A Quiet Place* are examples of such books.

A second means by which non-Afro-American writers create acceptable fiction about Afro-American experience is to place the characters within a setting that is very familiar to the author—one in which the author would have had contact with Afro-Americans. The authenticating details then can depict shared experience. Such a book is Robert Lipsyte's *The Contender*, which places its main character in the world of boxing, which Lipsyte knows intimately. Thus, because Lipsyte is also a skilled writer, he has created a believable character and a good book as well.

The same is true of books that focus on Black music, such as *Scat!* and *Ben's Trumpet*. The world of jazz music is one that is familiar to many non-Blacks who know and love and perform the music. These two books are also picture books and are therefore brief and relatively simple.

It is in the longer books set in the city, and in the books about growing up or about relationships among friends and within families, that the differences in perspective become most apparent. It is here that emphasis and authenticating detail mark the author's perspective as that of an outsider or an insider.

In the matter of emphasis, the problem is similar to that of the Peace Corps advertisement that asked whether a prospective volunteer saw a glass containing a quantity of liquid as half-empty or half-full. Both views were accurate, but the choice revealed something about the viewer's perspective on the world. So, too, does the depiction of Afro-American life experience, particularly urban experiences, reveal something about the perspective of an author.

Les Etter, in *Fast Break Forward*, probably best describes the half-empty view by stating through his narrator, "The writer who had named the Black Ghetto didn't need much imagination. It was a place of sudden violence, sordid poverty, and crime." And so it is—in *The Jazz Man*, that weird, dreamlike story in which a lame child is abandoned by his parents and nourished by jazz music; in *Durango Street*, where Rufus feels he must join a gang to survive; in *Trouble on Treat Street*; in *Member of the Gang*; in *Behind the Magic Line*. All of those books depict, with some degree of accuracy, some of the harsh reality of ghetto life. But their reality is that which can be seen by anyone who walks through a ghetto, or even by a regular visitor; it lacks the nuances apparent to those who call the ghetto home. The books miss out on the essence; they lose the substance by grasping at the shadow. What is minimized is the recognition that within those grim realities Afro-American people live their lives—they learn and grow and develop strength. They find sustenance in relationships with each other, and in their dreams, and in laughter.

Thus, even the grimmest of the city books by Afro-American authors (*A Hero Ain't Nothin' but a Sandwich* and *Teacup Full of Roses*) shine a bright spotlight on human relationships, on people reaching out to one another. The empty portion of the glass is recognized, but the emphasis is on the portion that is full.

The other dimension of the perspective problem is that of authenticating details. Most notable is the use, or misuse, of Black vernacular. Some authors simply have a tin ear for the style and grammar of Black speech. Bette Greene, in *Philip Hall Likes Me, I Reckon, Maybe*, tends to sprinkle the dialogue with random "You is" and "I is" constructions (and at least one insect, as in Reverend Ross's "Glory bee!"), which pass as rural Black vernacular. Anne Alexander, in *Trouble on Treat Street*, tends to sprinkle "be" constructions liberally and inaccurately throughout, such as, "We be thanking the Lord, Clem," as a description of an action to take place. Michelle Murray, in *Nellie Cameron*, shares the "be" habit.

In other places, the details simply lack credibility. Irene Hunt's *William* is a story in which a group of children—three Black and one white—become a family. The Black children are orphaned when their mother dies of cancer. The white girl, the oldest of the four, is an unwed mother who lives next door and who had been befriended by the children's mother. The book is set on the Gulf Coast. An Afro-American reader might question the unexplained absence of any of the Black children's relatives or, for that matter, any Black community, which leads to their fear of "orphan places"; the likelihood that Amy, the oldest Black child, would run off in a small southern town to live with her blond friend or that the people she would become closest to in school would be a group of white motorcyclists, whom she would invite to a party; and the likelihood that there would be no racial conflicts in such a setting. It is a warm story of love and loyalty, but it is unreal.

Another unreal story, at least for this writer, is Fitzhugh's *Nobody's Family Is Going to Change.* Given the well-known derogatory associations with the term *nigger*, especially from the mouths and pens of whites, how could she have a Black child call her brother "nigger Nijinsky"! Or this: "Emma couldn't say Daddy. It made her feel like a pickaninny in a bad movie running across a cotton field yelling 'Daddy, Daddy.'" Since when is *daddy* associated with pickaninnies? And where is the Black lawyer who, having achieved against heavy odds, would tell his Black wife that theatre people are trash when her brother is a professional dancer, her father has been in the theatre for forty years, and she herself has worked in the theatre? And where is the Black woman who would meekly accept that judgment? Where is the Black father who would laugh at the idea of his daughter being a lawyer? In any case, this story is overwhelmed by the number of issues it tries to handle—feminism, family relationships, children's rights, growing up, overeating. It is interesting to note that in the television film version called "That Dancing Kid," both the emphasis and the details were changed. It became the brother's story, not Emma's. The white maid is dropped. The dancing uncle becomes the father's brother and the father becomes his brother's former dancing partner, making their conflict more plausible.

Other inauthentic details vary from book to book. One example may clarify the point. In *Nellie Cameron*, the family attends the Zion A.M.E. Church. This particular A.M.E. church is not like any other known to one who grew up in that denomination. No television on Sunday? No spanking on Sunday? *Preacher* Evans? (A.M.E. ministers are usually called "Reverend.") And this: "Nellie liked standing up and hollering out the words about Jesus and Heaven and Precious Lord . . . all the fat ladies like Mama sighed and sweated . . . Mama shouted, 'Amen! Say it! That's surely the way it is!' . . . Shouting meant the end of the service." *Hollering* is not an accurate way to describe the singing of "Precious Lord." It is sung with much feeling, but never hollered. Shouting hardly signals the end of an A.M.E. church service. One could go on, but the point is made.

The image of "the fat ladies like Mama" sighing and sweating and shouting in church is similar to other images in certain of the culturally conscious books that raise questions about the authors' attitudes towards her characters. In *Philip Hall Likes Me, I Reckon, Maybe*, whose characters were classified as only superficially Black by *The Horn Book Magazine* (Heins, 1975), Beth's father, a turkey farmer, is unable to infer that his turkeys are being stolen by humans, not animals, and is also unable to reason that if he hides, he might be able to find out what is happening (Beth figures that out). He decides, therefore, to write to The Answer Man at a magazine to which he has had a "prescription" for fifteen years. And again we have the Amos-and-Andy image of a Black man using large words he does not know the meaning of. (Beth's sister also confuses "vegetarian" and "veterinarian.") On some level, it is easy to see why *Philip Hall Likes Me, I Reckon, Maybe* was a Newbery Honor Book. It is well written, and Beth is a smart, spirited, likeable hero. But it is difficult to understand why the author chose to make Beth and her family Black and thereby risked falling into the very traps she was unable to avoid.

In another example, it is hard not to wonder about the author's attitude toward her characters in *Behind the Magic Line* when she has one of them suggest to an old man that he could get a job— as a house*boy* or valet or butler: "You could look like that fellow on Uncle Ben's Rice." It is difficult to accept the image of the father of eight children (the youngest is born at the beginning of the book in a room in which the other seven are sleeping; they sleep through the birth) who simply disappears from time to time, who does not contact his family, and who then reappears to an ecstatic wife—she does not understand him, she just loves him.

A final example serves also as a recognition that not all of the flaws in questionable culturally conscious books are related to perspective. Some books are simply badly written. *Cockleburr Quarters* (Baker, 1972) combines the worst of both problems. It is a sentimental animal story written by someone with a tin ear for dialogue and with a condescending attitude toward Blacks. The family is composed of Mama, her five children, a live-in "uncle" who naps while Mama works, and a grandchild born to a fifteen-year-old who has quit school and who spends her time "washing and setting and spraying her hair," a decidedly non-Black way of characterizing a noncontributing teenager. Perhaps one quotation aptly sums up what appears to be the author's attitude toward the people she created: Dolph and the "mammy dog," Tory, "lay together in the sand, their bodies throbbing in sympathy. Tory's flesh and bones were covered with coarse dry hair. Dolph's were covered with smooth sooty skin. At the moment that seemed to be the only difference."

These examples indicate that realistic fiction supposedly depicting the Afro-American experience reflects both the author's individual perspectives and one of at least two different cultural perspectives. Within each of the two cultural perspectives, there is diversity; but with the possible exception of some picture books, it is almost always possible to identify the cultural perspective from which an author writes about Afro-American experience.

Characterizing Afro-American Experience

Within the culturally conscious books, as in the social conscience books and the melting pot books, certain recurring features mark the books as representative of that category. In terms of their power to reflect distinctly Afro-American experience, those features are handled more or less effectively, depending on the author's familiarity with the cultural milieu reflected in the books.

Language

As has been pointed out, language is the most easily distinguishable feature identifying a book that attempts to reflect on Afro-American experience. Black English appears in both dialogue and narration, although in some cases it does not appear at all.

The language of narrators and characters in the books is marked by distinctive grammar, lexicon, and style. It reflects the well-known syntactic features of Black English; for example, the absence of the copula, as in the statement "You think you bad" or in the title *My Brother Fine with Me;* or the ubiquitous "be," as pointed out in the previous section. Language also reflects Afro-American vocabulary: "I ain't *studyin'* about no white folks," or "toasty" as a label, or "nappy headed" as a description.

It should also be made clear that the linguistic markers of culturally conscious books are not limited to what some think of as "street slang" or "hip talk." Smitherman lists nine stylistic characteristics that she calls "rhetorical qualities of smaller individual units of expression" in Black language (p. 94). Among them are exaggerated language; that is, High (as in high-falutin') talk; mimicry—the adoption of another's voice, mannerism, or gestures when reporting on his or her speech; proverbial statements, such as "Cryin don't help nothin' except dirt in your eye"; punning and plays on words; image making and metaphor, as in "look like nine miles of bad road with a detour at the end"; braggadocio; and tonal semantics—the use of rhyme, rhythm, and repetitive sounds, as in Muhammed Ali's prefight "poems" (pp. 94–100).

While Black communicative styles do not appear in all the culturally conscious books, where they do appear they add richness and authenticity to the book. When done poorly, however, the attempt to represent Black dialect can reduce characters to caricatures.

Relationships between Young and Old

A number of the culturally conscious books feature a relationship between a very young person and someone at least two generations older. In some cases, the older person is a grandparent, as in the Mildred Taylor books and *Mr. Kelso's Lion*; or even a great-grandparent, as in *Cornrows* and *The Fastest Quitter in Town* (Green, 1972). In some books, the older person lives in the same household as the youngster; in others, they live separately. In a few instances, the two are not related at all.

The two most striking examples of this feature are *The Hundred Penny Box* and *Hi, Mrs. Mallory!* Aunt Dew, in *The Hundred Penny Box*, has a box in which she keeps a penny for each of the 100 years of her life. One of Michael's special joys is to count the pennies while his great-great-aunt relates stories about those years. In *Hi, Mrs. Mallory!*, Li'l Bits visits daily with her neighbor, Mrs. Mallory, who delights in telling stories as they sit around the pot-bellied stove. They share food, a love of going barefoot, and the affection of Mrs. Mallory's dogs. Mrs. Mallory also shares her mail (if it is addressed to Resident, it is for Li'l Bits), and Li'l Bits, in turn, writes checks for Mrs. Mallory.

Both *Raccoons Are for Loving* and *Lordy, Aunt Hattie* have a young girl enjoying a relationship with an older woman—grandmother or aunt. The stories of *The Lucky Stone* are told by Tee's great-grandmother, to whom she is especially close. In *The Fastest Quitter in Town*, it is only the young boy who is persistent enough to keep on looking for his great-grandfather's ring. Though he watches the old man's condition deteriorate, he refuses to participate in the grown-ups' deception and understands how much the ring means to his great-grandfather.

In only one of these books is the young person forced to deal with the death of the older one. The focus instead is on the special understanding that develops between the two. The older person is often teacher or mentor; the younger often helps with some task. The two have time, patience, and love to give to each other; and the result is a warm, close, honest, and satisfying relationship.

Extended Families

Somewhat related to the phenomenon of the young-old relationship is the shape of family units in many of the culturally conscious books. A few of the children in these books have been raised by grandparents—Ludell in *Ludell* and *Ludell and Willie*, Richard in *With My Face to the Rising Sun*, Tassie in *The Times They Used to Be*, Clem in *Trouble on Treat Street*.

Other stories are set in three-generation families: *The Lucky Stone, Sunflowers for Tina, Cornrows, A Hero Ain't Nothin but a Sandwich*. Interestingly, sometimes in those families the older person is not a grandparent, but a great-grandparent. In some books, the older person is somewhat weak and feeble; in others, an active, vital, contributing member of the household and one to whom the children are especially close.

These books also describe families with other relatives, such as aunts. And in a somewhat related phenomenon, some books include unrelated adults with whom children have a friendship— the janitor in *The Planet of Junior Brown* and Tweezer in *All Us Come Cross the Water*. Taken together, the young-old relationships and the extended families speak to a tradition of respect for older people within Afro-American families and communities and a traditional awareness of the ties that bind disparate members of those families and communities together.

Descriptions of Skin Color

The culturally conscious books provide an interesting contrast to the social conscience books in terms of the imagery used to describe the various skin colorings of Afro-Americans. While Huck (1979) suggests that such descriptions are unusual in children's fiction, they abound in the culturally conscious books. Gradations in skin color are almost automatically a part of an Afro-American's description of another Afro-American ("You remember her— light brown skinned, short Afro"), just as hair color is almost automatically a part of the description one Caucasian gives of another. In the social conscience books, the most frequent description of Afro-Americans is in terms of coffee, with cream for the more attractive. In the culturally conscious books, there are two interesting tendencies. One is to describe shading—light brown, reddish brown, dark brown, copper colored, olive, sandy brown, oak brown, light skinned. The other is to use positive (and often food-related) imagery to paint the person accurately—Hamilton's description of Zeely as "dark as a pole of Ceylon ebony" or James Baldwin's descriptions: skin like chocolate cake with no icing, or like watermelon and honey, or tea with milk, or black coffee first thing in the morning.

Such descriptions of skin color are indicative of an awareness of the naturalness of such descriptions among Afro-Americans and perhaps indicative of an effort to create and promote positive associations with the darkness that carries so many negative connotations in the English language.

Names, Nicknames, Terms of Address

Another of the recurring details that indicate an awareness of Afro-American traditions is naming. Some names are more likely to appear among certain groups than others. Ask an author to create a story about Bostonians or white Appalachians, and one would find that the character names are representative of the author's understanding of what would be typical for the locale. In the culturally conscious books, many authors choose names that reflect some understanding (or misunderstanding) of Afro-American naming traditions. Ludell, Tyree, Amifika, Lilly Etta, Arneatha, Butler, Elzie, Dewbet, Mattie Lee, are all names that would not be unexpected in an Afro-American household. (Note the absence of Rufus, Jasper, and Beulah.)

Nicknaming varies among cultural groups too, and the culturally conscious books recognize that fact. There is a tendency, especially among men and teenage boys, to provide nicknames that recall some incident, essential characteristic, or typical behavior of the person being named. Walter Dean Myers reflects this in his title *Fast Sam, Cool Clyde, and Stuff*, all of which are nicknames, the last for the character who bragged that he could "stuff" a basketball. One of the boys in *The Soul Brothers and Sister Lou* is nicknamed Fess, for Professor. A girl who wears glasses is called Blinky in *Little Man, Little Man.*

In some Afro-American families and communities, some terms of address are also traditional. Children are often referred to as "Baby" long after they are infants, as in "Come here, Baby, so I can comb your hair." Mothers are often called Mama, and grandmothers sometimes Big Mama. Siblings are often called Sister or Brother (or Bubba) within the family. Adults in the community are frequently referred to by Mr. or Miz and a first name, such as Mr. Larry. Traditionally, a child's response to an adult woman, or even an adult's response to a much older woman, included a "Ma'm." Examples of these terms of address abound in the culturally conscious books.

Afro-American Historical and Cultural Traditions

Many of the culturally conscious books, in addition to the ones that focus on Black heritage, include references to Afro-American historical events, traditions, and contributions. For example,

Louretta and her friends in *The Soul Brothers and Sister Lou* learn about the blues and soul music from Blind Eddie. Jazz music plays a role in several of the books. John Brown, in *Harlem Summer*, learns about Marcus Garvey, the Schomburg Library, talent night at the Apollo. M.C. Higgins learns of the history of escaping slaves.

Religious and Other Belief Systems

Many of the culturally conscious books include some reference to religion, church, and gospel music. Aunt Dew in *The Hundred Penny Box* sings "Precious Lord, take my hand. . . ." The funeral service in *The Soul Brothers and Sister Lou* is a traditional Black Baptist funeral service. Benjie's grandmother in *A Hero Ain't Nothin but a Sandwich* sees Jesus as her "waymaker" (who will make a way out of no way). Tassie's grandmother in *The Times They Used to Be* is sanctified. Ludell's grandmother and Edith Jackson's foster mother are both staunch churchgoers. While most of the characters who express strong religious beliefs are older women, there is recognition of the important role of religion and the church in the lives of Afro-Americans.

At the same time, there are a number of references in the culturally conscious books to non-Christian beliefs, such as the idea that a person "born with a veil over his eyes" has the gift of second sight, which appears in books by Lucille Clifton, Walter Dean Myers, and Sharon Bell Mathis. In *A Hero Ain't Nothin but a Sandwich* and in *A Long Day in November*, there are visits to conjure women. *Mojo and the Russians* is built on Dean's fear that Druscilla will "mojo" him, after he bumps into her with his bicycle. This seeming contradiction, which is simply a non-Western ability to accept two different belief systems simultaneously, is another component of Afro-American experience.

Conclusion

Of all the realistic fiction about Afro-Americans, the culturally conscious books seem most directly addressed to Black children as a primary audience. This is reflected, at least partly, in the choice of setting. The vast majority of these books are set in cities, a considerable number in the rural South, and very few in suburbs or small towns, corresponding to the general geographic distribution of the Black population of this country. A considerable number of the urban books present characters who have low incomes, which reflects another reality of Black life in America.

There is some question, however, about whether all of the culturally conscious books are talking *to* Black children or whether a few, like the social conscience books, do more talking *about* them; whether Black children are both subject and audience or merely subjects of some of these books. The question arises in relation to some of the specific details in some books, a few of which may be interpreted as derogatory, and in relation to the authors' choices of conditions and factors to emphasize—where they choose to shine their spotlights. The culturally conscious books are not free of ethnocentric outsiders' perspectives.

Where it seems clear that authors are attempting primarily to address Black children, to help them understand "how we got over," they have drawn on shared collective experiences and frames of reference to enrich their stories and enhance readers' opportunities to draw new insights. Obviously, this is done best by those who themselves have acquired those shared collective memories and that frame of reference through their own living.

A good story, well written and enriched with the specific details of living that make a cultural group distinctive, will naturally touch on the human universals extant within that cultural group. Such a story will be good literature, accessible to readers both inside and outside the group depicted. Thus, Afro-American children's fiction—the best of the culturally conscious books—adds a new and different dimension to the body of American children's literature.

The Culturally Conscious Books

African and "Down Home" Heritage and Traditions

Bontemps, Arna. *Mr. Kelso's Lion.* Illus. by Len Ebert. Philadelphia: J. B. Lippincott, 1970. (Gr. K-3)*

Bourne, Miriam. *Raccoons Are for Loving.* Illus. by Marian Morton. New York: Random House, 1968. (Preschool-Gr. 4)

Clifton, Lucille. *All Us Come Cross the Water.* Illus. by John Steptoe. New York: Holt, Rinehart and Winston, 1973. (Gr. K-4)

Clifton, Lucille. *The Lucky Stone.* Illus. by Dale Payson. New York: Delacorte Press, 1979. (Gr. 4-6)

Greenberg, Polly. *Oh Lord, I Wish I Was a Buzzard.* Illus. by Aliki. New York: Macmillan, 1968. (Gr. K-2)

Hamilton, Virginia. *The House of Dies Drear.* New York: Macmillan, 1968.

Steptoe, John. *Birthday.* New York: Holt, Rinehart and Winston, 1972. (Preschool-Gr. 3)

---

*Grade level designations from the 1979-1980 *Books in Print.*

Thomas, Ianthe. *Lordy, Aunt Hattie.* Illus. by Thomas DiGrazia. New York: Harper and Row, 1973. (Preschool-Gr. 3)

Yarbrough, Camille. *Cornrows.* Illus. by Carole Byard. New York: Coward, McCann and Geoghegan, 1979. (Gr. 2-5)

Common Everyday Experiences

Calloway, Northern J. (with Carol Hall). *I Been There.* Illus. by McLean Sammis. Garden City, N. Y.: Doubleday and Co., 1977. (Gr. K-1)

Greenfield, Eloise. *First Pink Light.* Illus. by Moneta Barnett. New York: Harper and Row, 1976. (Gr. K-3)

Myers, Walter Dean. *Fly, Jimmy, Fly.* Illus. by Moneta Barnett. New York: G. P. Putnam's Sons, 1974. (Gr. K-3)

Steptoe, John. *Stevie.* New York: Harper and Row, 1969. (Preschool-Gr. 3)

Steptoe, John. *Uptown.* New York: Harper and Row, 1970. (Gr. 3-5) O.P.**

Thomas, Dawn C. *Downtown Is.* Illus. by Colleen Browning. New York: McGraw-Hill, 1972. (Gr. 3-5) O.P.

Thomas, Ianthe. *Hi, Mrs. Mallory!* Illus. by Ann Toulmin-Rothe. New York: Harper and Row, 1979. (Gr. 2-5)

Surviving Racism and Discrimination

Graham, Lorenz. *Whose Town?* New York: Thomas Y. Crowell, 1969. (Gr. 5-up)

Screen, Robert. *With My Face to the Rising Sun.* New York: Harcourt Brace Jovanovich, 1977. (Gr. 7-up) O.P.

Shepard, Ray Anthony. *Sneakers.* New York: E. P. Dutton, 1973. (Gr. 5-8)

Taylor, Mildred. *Song of the Trees.* Illus. by Jerry Pinkney. New York: Dial Press, 1975. (Gr. 2-5)

Taylor, Mildred. *Roll of Thunder, Hear My Cry.* New York: Dial Press, 1976. (Gr. 6-up)

Living in the City

Agle, Nan Hayden. *Maple Street.* Illus. by Leonora Prince. New York: Seabury Press, 1970. (Gr. 3-7)

Alexander, Anne. *Trouble on Treat Street.* New York: Atheneum, 1974. (Gr. 4-6)

Baldwin, James. *Little Man, Little Man: A Story of Childhood.* Illus. by Yoran Cazac. New York: Dial Press, 1977. (Gr. 6-up)

Bonham, Frank. *Durango Street.* New York: E. P. Dutton, 1965. (Gr. 7-up)

Childress, Alice. *A Hero Ain't Nothin' but a Sandwich.* New York: Avon Books, 1974. (Gr. 7-up)

Deveaux, Alexis. *na-ni.* New York: Harper and Row, 1973. (Gr. 3-5) O.P.

Erwin, Betty K. *Behind the Magic Line.* Boston: Little, Brown and Co., 1969. (Gr. 3-7)

**O.P. = Out of Print.

Fox, Paula. *How Many Miles to Babylon.* Illus. by Paul Giovanopoulos. New York: David White, 1967. (Gr. 5-8)

Hunter, Kristin. *The Soul Brothers and Sister Lou.* New York: Charles Scribner's Sons, 1968. (Gr. 7-up)

Jordan, June. *His Own Where.* New York: T. Y. Crowell, 1971. (Gr. 7-up)

King, Helen H. *Willy.* Illus. by Carole Byard. Garden City, N. Y.: Doubleday and Co., 1971. (Gr. 3-5) O.P.

Lipsyte, Robert. *The Contender.* New York: Harper and Row, 1967. (Gr. 8-up)

Mathis, Sharon. *Sidewalk Story.* Illus. by Leo Carty. New York: Viking Press, 1971. (Gr. 2-4)

Mathis, Sharon. *Teacup Full of Roses.* New York: Viking Press, 1972. (Gr. 8-up)

Myers, Walter Dean. *The Dancers.* Illus. by Anne Rockwell. New York: Parents Magazine Press, 1972. (Gr. K-3)

Myers, Walter Dean. *It Ain't All for Nothin.* New York: Viking Press, 1978. (Gr. 8-up)

Myers, Walter Dean. *The Young Landlords.* New York: Viking Press, 1979. (Gr. 7-up)

Rinkoff, Barbara. *Member of the Gang.* New York: Crown Publishers, 1968. (Gr. 4-6)

Vroman, Mary Elizabeth. *Harlem Summer.* New York: G. P. Putnam's Sons, 1967. (Gr. 6-up)

Weik, Mary Hays. *The Jazz Man.* Illus. by Ann Grifalconi. New York: Atheneum, 1966. (Gr. 2-up)

Friendships and Peer Relationships

Brown, Margery. *That Ruby.* Chicago: Reilly and Lee, 1969. (Gr. 4-6) O.P.

Clifton, Lucille. *Three Wishes.* Illus. by Stephanie Douglas. New York: Viking Press, 1974. (Gr. K-3)

Clifton, Lucille. *The Times They Used to Be.* Illus. by Susan Jeschke. New York: Dell, 1974. (Gr. 3-5)

Fife, Dale. *Who Goes There, Lincoln?* Illus. by Paul Galdone. New York: Coward, McCann and Geoghegan, 1975. (Gr. 2-5)

Guy, Rosa. *The Friends.* New York: Holt, Rinehart and Winston, 1973. (Gr. 7-up)

Hamilton, Virginia. *The Planet of Junior Brown.* New York: Macmillan, 1971. (Gr. 6-up)

Hunt, Irene. *William.* New York: Charles Scribner's Sons, 1977. (Gr. 5-up)

King, Helen. *The Soul of Christmas.* Illus. by Fred Anderson. Chicago: Johnson Publishing Co., 1972. (Gr. K-4)

Myers, Walter Dean. *Fast Sam, Cool Clyde, and Stuff.* New York: Viking Press, 1975. (Gr. 5-up)

Myers, Walter Dean. *Mojo and the Russians.* New York: Viking Press, 1977. (Gr. 6-up)

Family Relationships

Cavin, Ruth. *Timothy, the Terror.* Illus. by Jean-Jacques Loup. New York: Harlin Quist Books, 1972. (Gr. 1–3)

Clifton, Lucille. *My Brother Fine with Me.* Illus. by Moneta Barnett. New York: Holt, Rinehart and Winston, 1975. (Gr. K–3)

Clifton, Lucille. *Amifika.* Illus. by Thomas DiGrazia. New York: E. P. Dutton, 1977. (Preschool–Gr. 2)

Fitzhugh, Louise. *Nobody's Family Is Going to Change.* New York: Farrar, Strauss, and Giroux, 1974. (Gr. 3–7)

Gaines, Ernest J. *A Long Day in November.* New York: Dell, 1971. (Gr. 4–6)

Greenfield, Eloise. *Good News.* Illus. by Pat Cummings. New York: Coward, McCann and Geoghegan, 1977. Originally published as *Bubbles,* 1972. (Gr. K–3)

Greenfield, Eloise. *She Come Bringing Me That Little Baby Girl.* Illus. by John Steptoe. Philadelphia: J. B. Lippincott, 1974. (Gr. K–3)

Greenfield, Eloise. *Sister.* New York: Thomas Y. Crowell, 1974. (Gr. 5–12)

Greenfield, Eloise. *Talk about a Family.* Illus. by James Calvin. Philadelphia: J. B. Lippincott, 1978. (Gr. 5–8)

Hunter, Kristin. *Boss Cat.* Illus. by Harold Franklin. New York: Charles Scribner's Sons, 1971. (Gr. 2–5)

Jordan, June. *New Life, New Room.* Illus. by Ray Cruz. New York: Thomas Y. Crowell, 1975. (Gr. 3–5)

Lexau, Joan M. *Striped Ice Cream.* Illus. by John Wilson. Philadelphia: J. B. Lippincott, 1968. (Gr. 2–6)

Mathis, Sharon Bell. *The Hundred Penny Box.* Illus. by Leo and Diane Dillon. New York: Viking Press, 1975. (Gr. K–3)

Prather, Ray. *Anthony and Sabrina.* New York: Macmillan, 1973. (Gr. K–3)

Growing Up and Finding Oneself

Baker, Charlotte. *Cockleburr Quarters.* Englewood Cliffs, N. J.: Prentice Hall, 1972. (Gr. 3–7)

Baldwin, Anne Norris. *Sunflowers for Tina.* Illus. by Ann Grifalconi. New York: Four Winds Press, 1970. (Gr. K–3)

Blue, Rose. *A Quiet Place.* Illus. by Tom Feelings. New York: Franklin Watts, 1969. (Gr. 4–6)

Clifton, Lucille. *The Boy Who Didn't Believe in Spring.* Illus. by Brinton Turkle. New York: E. P. Dutton, 1973. (Gr. 3–4)

Dobrin, Arnold. *Scat!* New York: Four Winds Press, 1971. (Gr. K–3)

Etter, Les. *Fast Break Forward.* New York: Hastings House, 1969. (Gr. 6–9)

Gray, Genevieve. *Send Wendell.* Illus. by Symeon Shimin. New York: McGraw-Hill, 1974. (Preschool–Gr. 4)

Green, Phyllis. *The Fastest Quitter in Town.* Illus. by Lorenzo Lynch. New York: Young Scott Books, 1972. (Gr. 1–4)

Greene, Bette. *Philip Hall Likes Me, I Reckon, Maybe.* Illus. by Charles Lilly. New York: Dial Press, 1974. (Gr. 3–6)

Grimes, Nikki. *Growin'*. Illus. by Charles Lilly. New York: Dial Press, 1977. (Gr. 3-6)

Guy, Rosa. *Edith Jackson*. New York: Viking Press, 1978. (Gr. 7-up)

Hamilton, Virginia. *Zeely*. New York: Macmillan, 1967. (Gr. 4-6)

Hamilton, Virginia. *M.C. Higgins, the Great*. New York: Macmillan, 1974. (Gr. 5-up)

Hamilton, Virginia. *Arilla Sun Down*. New York: Greenwillow Books, 1976. (Gr. 7-up)

Isadora, Rachel. *Ben's Trumpet*. New York: Greenwillow Books, 1979. (Gr. K-3)

Jackson, Jesse. *Tessie*. New York: Harper and Row, 1968. (Gr. 4-8)

Little, Lessie Jones, and Greenfield, Eloise. *I Can Do It by Myself*. Illus. by Carole Byard. New York: Thomas Y. Crowell, 1978. (Gr. K-2)

Mathis, Sharon Bell. *Listen for the Fig Tree*. New York: Viking Press, 1974. (Gr. 7-up)

Molarsky, Osmond. *Song of the Empty Bottles*. Illus. by Tom Feelings. New York: Henry Z. Walck, 1968. (Gr. 4-7)

Murray, Michelle. *Nellie Cameron*. Illus. by Leonora Prince. New York: Seabury Press, 1971. (Gr. 3-6)

Steptoe, John. *Marcia*. New York: Viking Press, 1976. (Gr. 7-up)

Walter, Mildred Pitts. *Lillie of Watts*. Illus. by Leonora Prince. Pasadena, Calif.: Ward Ritchie Press, 1969. (Gr. 3-5) O.P.

Wilkinson, Brenda. *Ludell*. New York: Harper and Row, 1975. (Gr. 5-up)

Wilkinson, Brenda. *Ludell and Willie*. New York: Harper and Row, 1977. (Gr. 5-up)

5 The Image-Makers

Can I get a witness?

Traditional Call for a Confirming
Response—Black Churches

In the first chapter, James Baldwin was quoted as asserting that an author "writes to change the world" by altering the way people look at reality. In that same interview, he referred to the writer as "a witness." Thus the writer, in Baldwin's view, becomes the one who not only sees, but who also confirms for others what they, too, have perceived and understood. The writer-witness translates and transforms reality, and then holds the result up for other witnesses to confirm.

The writer-witnesses who have produced the books in this survey, it can be assumed, were attempting to change the world, at least the all-white world of children's books, by creating truer images of Afro-Americans and by increasing their visibility. It has been argued that potentially the most successful of those efforts have been the culturally conscious books.

The people whose souls have been witnesses to Afro-American experience have been those who, in Virginia Hamilton's phrase, have "dared to live" it. Of the eighty-nine culturally conscious books in the survey, sixty-five were produced by Black authors. Of those sixty-five, twenty-eight (40 percent) were produced by just five people. Although twenty-nine other Black authors are represented in the total survey, it can be argued that these five have made a substantial contribution to the image of Afro-Americans in children's fiction that has appeared since 1965. Because theirs has been a major contribution, this chapter is devoted to an overview of the work of these five authors and a brief analysis of the common themes and emphases that make their work distinctive. In alphabetical order, the authors are Lucille Clifton, Eloise Greenfield, Virginia Hamilton, Sharon Bell Mathis, and Walter Dean Myers. The chapter also includes a brief discussion of the work of a few other important Black authors and illustrators.

Lucille Clifton

Named Poet Laureate of Maryland in 1979, Lucille Clifton writes for both adults and children. She has published four volumes of poetry for adults. The first, *Good Times*, was named one of the ten best books in 1969 by the *New York Times;* the most recent, *Two-Headed Woman*, was awarded the 1980 Juniper Prize by the University of Massachusetts Press. Clifton has also written a family history, *Generations: A Memoir*. Born in Depew, New York, she now lives in Baltimore with her family.

In her role as image-maker, Clifton presents her readers with Black children who are strong, spirited, irrepressible. They are certainly believable, probably because Clifton, the mother of six, knows something about how children think and behave, as well as what their questions and concerns are.

Clifton's first published children's book was *Some of the Days of Everett Anderson* (1970), which relates Everett Anderson's adventures in the form of poetry. He is an irresistible, ebony six-year-old who is full of tricks and full of joy. Everett Anderson appears in five other books. In the early ones, he and his mother are a happy, loving family, even though Everett spends some of his time waiting for her to come home from work and some time missing his father, whom he remembers with love. In the most recent of the Everett Anderson books, *Everett Anderson's Nine Month Long* (1978), his mother has remarried, and by the end of the book, Everett has a new baby sister.

Another of Clifton's poetic picture books, *Good, Says Jerome* (1973), recognizes some of the things that can be frightening for young children. In the form of a dialogue between a brother and a sister, this book provides reassuring answers: "I don't want to move./ Oh, Jerome . . ./ we are us/ wherever we are,/ if we live right here or/ go away far/ we'll have old memories/ and new friends./ Good,/ says Jerome/ I thought beginnings/ were ends."

Two of her picture books focus on African and Afro-American heritage—*The Black BC's* (1970), an informative "alphabet book" that tells of contributions of Blacks, and *All Us Come Cross the Water* (1973) in which Ujamaa seeks, and finds, the answer to "where did we come from?"

Two other books recall, in flashbacks, earlier times. In *The Times They Used to Be* (1974), Mama (Sooky) tells a story about the summer of 1948 when she was twelve and her best friend Tassie had "sin" break out all over her body because she was not saved. It was also the summer that television came to the local hardware store, and Sooky's Uncle Sunny, veteran of the all-colored 92nd Division, followed a nun-ghost off the Grider Street Bridge to his death. *The Lucky Stone* (1979) traces, through stories told by Tee's great-grandmother, Elzie Free Pickens, the history of a lucky black stone that has been handed down since the days of slavery.

Clifton's other books are about contemporary Black children, who invariably are lively, likeable, independent, spunky. There is Desire Mary Tate, the four-year-old in *Don't You Remember?* (1973). *She* remembers and is angry when her family forgets their promises, until her birthday when *they* remember, even though apparently she forgot. There is also King Shabazz, in *The Boy Who Didn't Believe in Spring* (1973); he takes his friend Tony Polito on a quest for this elusive thing called spring, which people keep insisting is "just around the corner" but which, as far as he could see, is nonexistent. In *The Three Wishes* (1976) Zenobia believes that the penny she found with her birth year on it will bring good luck in the form of three wishes. She is convinced of her good luck when she temporarily loses, then regains, the friendship of her neighbor, Victorius, just as she wishes. The title character in *Amifika* (1977) overhears a conversation between Mama and Aunt Kate in which they mention getting rid of something to make more room for Daddy, who is returning home from the Army. Deciding that he, Amifika, is what they will get rid of, he hides. They will have to find him to get rid of him. He falls asleep and wakes up to the sounds of a joyful reunited family. Baggy, in *My Brother Fine with Me* (1975), has decided to run away. His sister, Johnetta, helps him get his things together, since she can be the only child again if he runs away. When he is gone, she misses him and is happy to discover that he has run only as far as the front steps.

The fictional Clifton children, almost all of whom appear in picture books, have been brought to life by a number of different illustrators. Some, such as Brinton Turkle, Ann Grifalconi, and Evaline Ness, are well-established children's book illustrators. Others, such as Black illustrators Stephanie Douglas and Moneta Barnett, are less widely known. All have succeeded in capturing the liveliness of the children and the varying moods of their stories. Combined with Clifton's poetry or lyrical prose, they have created a memorable body of work.

Clifton's children's books are clearly "upbeat." She seems to take seriously a line from her poem "Good Times": "Oh, children, think about the good times." These are not children to whom "being born a Negro" does something harmful, as the social worker in *A New Home for Theresa* asserted. There is no pathology of race or culture in the Clifton books. On the contrary, feeling good about being Black is one of the threads that run through Clifton's books. It is strongest in the "heritage" books—*The Black BC's* and *All Us Come Cross the Water*—but it is also apparent in the easy references to being Black in the Everett Anderson books— "somebody brown and warm and sweet," "Daddy's back is broad and black," and "Who's black and runs and loves to hop? Ebony Everett Anderson." Perhaps this feeling is best expressed in *Good, Says Jerome*: "Black is a color/ like yellow or white./ It's got nothing to do/ with wrong or right./ It's a feeling inside/ about who we are and/ how strong and how free./ Good/ says Jerome/ that feels like me."

Clifton's pride in being Black does not prevent her from including interracial friendships in her books. Jacob in *My Friend Jacob* (1980) is white; his friend Sam is Black. Tony Polito in *The Boy Who Didn't Believe in Spring* is also white. However, in both these books, Clifton makes it clear that the Black boy is the leader.

Her vision of Afro-American experience is also broad enough for Clifton to include a variety of language styles in her books. She is equally at home with poetry (the Everett Anderson books), standard English (*Don't You Remember?*), and Black vernacular (*My Brother Fine with Me*).

Uppermost in Lucille Clifton's fictional Afro-American experience is an emphasis on the importance of human relationships, or, as stated in her nonfiction work, *Generations: A Memoir*, an emphasis on the lines that "connect in thin ways that last and last" (Clifton, 1976, p. 78). There is, in all of her books, a strong emphasis on family ties, on love, and on the small shared experiences that hold family and friends together.

The other aspect of human relationships that is strong in the Clifton books is a sense of continuity. It shows most directly in *All Us Come Cross the Water* and in *The Lucky Stone*. In *The Times They Used to Be*, this continuity is illustrated in the scene at the funeral home when Tassie "comes into her nature" and Sooky's mother whispers to her dead brother, "Oh Sunny Jim, . . . it's a sign all right. . . . Life keeps on, you know." That spirit of survival and of celebration of family, in both the narrow kinship sense and in the broad community sense ("When the colored people came to Depew they came to be a family. . . . The generations of white folks are just people but the generations of colored folks are families" [Clifton, 1976, p. 64]), is the spirit of her books, and is best expressed in this, the penultimate passage from *Generations*:

Things don't fall apart. Things hold. Lines connect in thin ways that last and last and lives become generations made out of pictures and words just kept. "We come out of it better than they did, Lue," my Daddy said, and I watch my six children and know we did. They walk with confidence through the world, free sons and daughters of free folk, for my Mama told me slavery was a temporary thing, mostly we was free and she was right. And she smiled when she said it and Daddy smiled too and saw that my sons are as strong as my daughters and it had been made right.

And I could tell you about things we been through, some awful ones, some wonderful, but I know that the things that made us are more than that, our lives are more than that, our lives are more than the days in them, our lives are our line and we go on. [Pp. 78-79]

For a complete listing of the books by Lucille Clifton discussed in this section, see pages 99-100.

Eloise Greenfield

Born in Parmele, North Carolina, Eloise Greenfield moved when she was young to Washington, D. C., where she currently lives with her family. To date, she has published thirteen children's books, including three biographies, a book of poems, and a "three-generation memoir." She also has published a number of short stories and articles. Her two most recent books have been co-authored with her mother, Lessie Jones Little. During the early 1970s, Greenfield was a member of the now-defunct D.C. Black Writer's Workshop, a group that also included Sharon Bell Mathis. The group was devoted to encouraging the writing and publishing of Black literature.

Her own desires for her readers are clearly expressed in an article in *The Horn Book Magazine* entitled "Something to Shout About" (1975). Because they parallel the apparent aims of much Black-produced children's literature and because they are reflected so clearly in her books, these desires are paraphrased and repeated here. She wrote of trying, through her books, to sustain children by (1) giving them a love of the arts, (2) encouraging them to hold positive attitudes towards themselves, (3) presenting them with alternative methods for coping with the negative aspects of their lives, (4) giving them an appreciation for the contributions of their elders, (5) providing true knowledge of Black (African and American) heritage, (6) allowing them to fall in love with Black heroes, (7) reflecting and reinforcing positive aspects of their lives, and (8) sharing her own love of words.

While all of these aims are reflected in her books, some are expressed more obviously and directly than others. Her three biographies, all part of the Crowell Biography Series, best demonstrate her success in carrying out these objectives. She presents three Black heroes with whom children have an opportunity to "fall in love." The first was *Rosa Parks* (1973), the story of the "Mother of the Civil Rights Movement," whose refusal to give up her seat on a bus triggered the Montgomery bus boycott and Martin Luther King Jr.'s assumption of a leadership role. The other two biographies are portraits of Paul Robeson (1975), the late singer, actor, athlete, and rights activist; and Mary McLeod Bethune (1977), the educator who almost single-handedly built Bethune-Cookman College. As are all the biographies in the Crowell series, these books are written in an easy-to-read style and are therefore accessible to a wide range of readers. They stress the strengths that enabled their subjects to achieve and are honest in portraying conditions that had to be overcome.

A direct effort to provide some knowledge of Black heritage is found in *Africa Dream* (1977) in which a young girl dreams of a journey to ancient Africa. The dream permits Greenfield to present information about the African heritage of Black Americans.

Honey I Love and Other Poems (1978), a delightful book that is beautifully illustrated by Leo and Diane Dillon, exhibits her desire to share with children her own love of words. It also includes at least one hero, Harriet Tubman. The theme of this book of poetry focuses on what she considers one of the positive aspects of Black children's lives, love—"Love is a staple in most Black families" (Greenfield, 1975, p. 626)—including self-love.

Her most recent book, *Childtimes: A Three Generation Memoir* (1979) is co-authored with her mother and contains material by her grandmother. The introduction to *Childtimes* echoes the same spirit expressed in Lucille Clifton's books:

> This book is about family. Kinsfolk touching across the centuries, walking with one hand clasping the hands of those who have gone before, the other hand reaching back for those who will come after.
>
> This book, most of all, is about black people struggling, not just to stay alive, but to live, to give of their talents, whether to many or few. Through all of their pain and grief, and even their mistakes, black people have kept on going, had some good times, given a lot of love to one another, and never stopped trying to help their children get on board the freedom train.
>
> There's a lot of crying in this book, and there's dying, too, but there's also new life and laughter. It's all part of living. [P. ix]

Greenfield's realistic fiction, too, is about family and about Black children learning to live, continuing on through pain and grief, having some good times, and giving a lot of love to one another. Unlike Clifton, Greenfield has so far created only Afro-American major characters. However, like Clifton, her reflections of Afro-American experience are not monolithic. She too varies her language from poetry to standard English to Black vernacular. The shape of her families varies as well, and in the two novels we find again the availability of an older person to be a sounding board offering advice and support to the young.

In the books for younger children, Greenfield also accomplishes her objectives, but the tone is much lighter than in the quotation from *Childtimes*. *Good News* (formerly *Bubbles*, 1972) features James Edward, who feels "warm and glowy all the way from his inside self to his outside brownness" because he can read. He is eager to share his good news with his mother but is disappointed when she is too busy to listen. However, he shares his news with his baby sister, whose obvious affection and need for him provides support and bolsters his spirit and his confidence in himself. Maybe by tomorrow his reading repertoire will have expanded from three words to five—or six! A similar story, *She Come Bringing Me That Little Baby Girl* (1974), tells of Kevin's disappointment in the baby girl who arrives in spite of his request for a baby brother with whom he could play ball. But when his mother explains that she needs his help to take care of the baby and that she herself was once a baby girl who was cared for by Uncle Roy, the baby begins to look better to Kevin.

Me and Nessie (1975) and *I Can Do It by Myself* (1978) also portray a young child who is gaining some maturity. In *Me and Nessie*, Janell realizes that as she goes off to school and has new experiences, she will no longer need Nessie, her imaginary friend. *I Can Do It by Myself*, Greenfield's other collaboration with Lessie Jones Little, features Donny, who has saved a dollar. He succeeds in going to the store, purchasing his mother's birthday plant, and surviving an encounter with a frightful bulldog—all by himself.

In *First Pink Light* (1976), Tyree decides to stay up all night to wait for the return of his father, who has been away for a month taking care of Grandmother. His wise mother suggests that he put on his pajamas and wait in the big chair until the first pink light of dawn, when he can hide to surprise his father. He falls asleep, of course, and does not even open his eyes when the man with the "strong brown face" carries him off to bed.

Greenfield's two junior novels, *Sister* (1974) and *Talk about a Family* (1978), feature young women learning to cope with some hard times within their families and their lives. Sister records her story in her memory book, which was given to her by her father before he died. Greenfield (1975) says of *Sister*, "Sister, who is Doretha, discovers that she can use her good times as stepping stones, as bridges, to get over the hard times—the death of her father, the alienation of her older sister, her struggles with school work" (p. 625). Genny, in *Talk about a Family*, must face the breakup of her family. In an interview with Rosalie B. Kiah (1980), Greenfield discussed the theme of this novel: "Families come in various shapes. . . . All of them are legitimate. In the case of divorce and separation . . . the children can go on and build their lives regardless of the problems of the parents. Children *have* to go on and build their lives" (p. 658). Genny's family becomes two circles linked together—"Me and Kim and Mac and Larry and Mama; Me and Kim and Mac and Larry and Daddy."

Greenfield's fictional children, like Clifton's, are strong and resilient. They are self-confident and, when faced with problems, are able to find support in the good times and in the love of their families.

For a complete listing of the books by Eloise Greenfield discussed in this section, see page 100.

Virginia Hamilton

Virginia Hamilton is possessed of an imagination as fertile as the Ohio farmland on which her extended family, the Perrys, grew and flourished. She was the granddaughter of an escaped slave, the daughter of a Black man who achieved what was almost unheard of for a Black—a college degree in business in the 1890s—and then saw his career dreams go unfulfilled. Hamilton still lives in Yellow Springs, Ohio, the area in which she grew up. She is married to Arnold Adoff (a writer, poet, and anthologist) and is the mother of two children.

Hamilton is the most daring of the writers represented in the survey and among the most skilled writers of contemporary children's literature. Her books are often multilayered, multifaceted, full of symbols, and deep enough to be mined again and again for new insights or just savored for the quality of her imagination. Her willingness to take risks also results, in each of her books, in a touch of the unusual, the eccentric, perhaps even the bizarre— a 262-pound musical prodigy who plays a silent piano, a boy sitting and swaying on top of a forty-foot pole near the top of a mountain, a six and one-half foot tall pigkeeper who looks like a Watusi queen. From her father's stories about Paul Robeson, Hamilton absorbed the impression that "if one were to become anything, it would have to be not only the best, but wholly original, a new idea. I grew up yearning for the unusual, seeking something unique in myself. I longed, not only to write, but to newly write, and like no one else. Kenneth Hamilton wanted no less for his youngest child" (Hamilton, 1974, p. xiv). Kenneth Hamilton would not be disappointed.

Virginia Hamilton's five realistic novels are all steeped in her own experiences and those of her family and her people, though she also stated, in her Newbery Award acceptance speech, that she has "never written demonstrable and classifiable truths" (1975b). Her work is not autobiographical in any direct sense. Earlier, in an article called "High John Is Risen Again" (1975a), she had said of her work: "What I am compelled to write can best be described as some essence of the dreams, lies, myths, and disasters befallen a clan of my blood relatives. . . . Some essence, then, of their language and feeling, which through space-time imagery I project as the unquenchable spirit of a whole people" (p. 118).

This focus on "the unquenchable spirit of a whole people" is an echo of the emphasis on the positive aspects of growing up Afro-American that is found in the work of Clifton, Greenfield, and other Black authors. In Hamilton's realistic fiction, the dreams, lies, and myths, as well as the truths of her heritage, are woven into the fabric of the stories—sometimes a major part of the design, sometimes background against which the design is etched.

Elizabeth Perry, the eleven-year-old in *Zeely* (1967), sees a portrait of a Watusi queen in a magazine, which sets her imagination soaring. Elizabeth, who has become Geeder for the summer, fantasizes that Zeely Taber, six and one-half feet tall and "dark as a pole of Ceylon ebony," is also a Watusi queen. Geeder has seen Zeely walking at night and has frightened her brother with stories about the night traveler. When he asks Uncle Ross about night travelers, he learns of the songs of escaping slaves and prisoners—"night travelers who meant to walk tall and be free." Zeely herself, through a discussion and a myth, helps Geeder to see the importance of being herself. She also encourages her to hold on to her own way of dreaming, while not losing touch with reality. Elizabeth realizes that Zeely really is a queen, because of her pride and dignity and free spirit.

The House of Dies Drear (1970) is a mystery story. The house had once been a station on the Underground Railroad. Dies Drear, who had owned the house, was murdered, as were two slaves who had been hiding there. Their ghosts are rumored to haunt the house. The house is currently being cared for by a strange old man called Mr. Pluto. When the Smalls family moves into the house, strange and mysterious things begin to happen. Thomas Smalls becomes caught up in the mystery and, in the process of solving it, learns much about the history of the Underground Railroad.

The Planet of Junior Brown (1972) moves the setting from Ohio to New York, where Hamilton lived for a while. Junior, a 262-pound musical genius, is befriended by street-wise Buddy Clark and Mr. Poole, a teacher-turned-janitor. Buddy has no home and is the Tomorrow Billy for a "solar system" of urban "planets"—abandoned buildings where groups of homeless boys survive. Mr. Poole has built a model solar system in a secret room in the basement of the junior high school. Instead of attending classes, Junior and Buddy hang out with Mr. Poole. They are caught, and Mr. Poole must dismantle his solar system. By that time, Junior Brown has been overtaken by his life and his fantasies (his asthmatic mother, who has silenced his piano, and his music teacher's ghost relative), and Buddy must find a planet for Junior and for Mr. Poole's solar system, which includes a large special planet— the planet of Junior Brown. "We are together because we have to learn to live for each other." Together they will survive.

M.C. Higgins, the Great (1974) presents another survival problem. Seated atop his forty-foot pole, which he won by swimming the Ohio River, M.C. surveys his world and wonders how to save Sarah's Mountain from the strip-mining spoil heap that threatens to come crashing down on his home and family. Sarah's Mountain was named after M.C.'s slave ancestor who, like Hamilton's Grandfather Perry, escaped to Ohio. All Sarah's descendants are living on or buried on the mountain. In his desperation, M.C. dreams that a dude collecting folk songs will hear his mother, Banina Higgins, sing, and will take them all away and make her a star. His world, which includes a friendship with a family his father thinks is "witchy," is also entered by a wandering teenage girl who stays just long enough to help M.C. learn something about his own responsibility for making choices and decisions. In the end, M.C. realizes that he himself must take some action to save himself and his family.

Arilla Sun Down (1976) incorporates another aspect of Hamilton's heritage. She, like Arilla, has some Native American ancestry and is part of an interracial family. Arilla's father is part

Black, part Indian; her mother is Black. Her brother is determined to be the ultimate "Amerind." Arilla begins the year feeling as if she is "dangling at the end of a rope and not being able to let go." By the end of the novel, she has begun to find her own identity and is comfortable with herself and her family. *Arilla Sun Down* is not an easy book to read. Its language is impressionistic. It is full of flashbacks and symbols—most notably the never-ending circle, a symbol of continuity. In all, it is rather unconventional children's literature.

Written during the same time period as Hamilton's realistic fiction were the two Jahdu books, *The Time-Ago Tales of Jahdu* (1969) and *Time-Ago Lost: More Tales of Jahdu* (1973). Both are set in Harlem and involve Mama Luka, who pulls Jahdu stories out of the air to tell to James Edward, whom she cares for while his parents are at work. The books are a mixture of fantasy and realism. They are fablelike, and through them James Edward acquires insights into himself and life in general.

The most recent of Hamilton's books involve a fantasy cycle that centers on Justice, her twin brothers Levi and Thomas, and a neighbor boy. All have psychic powers that will apparently allow them to survive into the far distant future. In the first book, *Justice and Her Brothers* (1978), Justice discovers her own psychic powers. In *Dustland* (1980), the four children, as The Unit, move in and out of time and space to explore a future place, Dustland. The recently released *The Gathering* (1980) is the third book in the series.

Hamilton has also produced three books of nonfiction: a biography of W.E.B. DuBois (1972), an edited collection of the writings of DuBois (1975), and a biography of Paul Robeson (1974). DuBois and Robeson were two of the radical Black heroes about whom Kenneth Hamilton taught his children, and Virginia Hamilton wanted young readers to know about their lives.

Whether fantasy, fiction, or biography, Hamilton writes about survivors. Her fantasy books move away from her personal heritage, but they continue the survival theme. Her realistic fiction, like some of the works of Clifton and Greenfield, stresses her heritage and, through it, the heritage and essence of a people. She, like Clifton and Greenfield, also stresses continuity—the circle in *Arilla Sun Down*, the legacy of *Dies Drear*, the circle that begins and ends with Sarah in *M.C. Higgins, the Great*. And while she plays with space-time imagery, she also stresses human emotions, human relationships, and human connections.

For a complete listing of the books by Virginia Hamilton discussed in this section, see pages 100–101.

Sharon Bell Mathis

Sharon Bell Mathis was born in Atlantic City, New Jersey, and grew up in Brooklyn, New York. Formerly the head of the children's division of the D.C. Black Writer's Workshop and for several years a special education teacher, she currently lives in Washington, D.C.

Mathis says that she "writes to salute Black kids." In contrast to Hamilton, Clifton, and Greenfield, some of Mathis's novels include harsh realities, but she also celebrates the strengths that have enabled Black people to survive these realities. In *Listen for the Fig Tree* (1974), her attitude is expressed through Muffin's thoughts at a Kwanza celebration: "To be Black was to be strong, to have courage, to survive. And it wasn't an alone thing. It was family." The remainder of that passage makes it clear that "family" is again used in the broad sense that includes not only kin, but friends and the community of Blacks.

Mathis salutes the blind musician Ray Charles (1973) in a contribution to the Crowell Biography Series, a book that is brief and written simply. Mathis said on the flyleaf of the book, "The triumphs of Ray Charles are the triumphs of all Black people—a story of great will, of great strength, and a profound sense of survival." Those are the qualities she tends to focus on in her fiction.

One of Mathis's earliest books, *Sidewalk Story* (1971), won first prize in the Minority Writers Contest of the Council on Interracial Books for Children. It focuses on the friendship between nine-year-old Lilly Etta and Tanya Brown. Tanya's family is being evicted because they are behind in paying the rent. Their furniture is placed on the sidewalk, and Lilly Etta is incensed. Lilly Etta's mother, who is dependent on "the city" for her income, feels she cannot help. Lilly Etta, remembering that publicity had helped another evicted tenant, calls first the police and then the newspaper for help. None seems forthcoming, and the Browns' furniture remains on the sidewalk. That night, when rain threatens, Lilly Etta tries single-handedly, with her mother's sheets and blankets, to keep the furniture dry. As she sleeps atop the furniture in the rain, the reporter she spoke with arrives on the scene. The resulting publicity brings offers of help for Tanya's family and a box of gold earrings to replace the straws in Lilly Etta's ears. There is strong emphasis on the fact that it was Lilly Etta's will to act that made the difference. While both families have little money, which is the reason for the Browns' eviction, the spotlight is on the friendship between the girls and Lilly Etta's determination.

Another determined nine-year-old, Michael Jefferson, takes on the task of saving from destruction the old, beat-up box in which Aunt Dew keeps her hundred pennies, one for each year of her life. She is Michael's great-great aunt, who raised Michael's father after he was orphaned and who has now been brought from Atlanta to live with the family. She shares Michael's room, and they have a close, loving relationship. Michael counts the pennies while Aunt Dew recites the history of each year. Aunt Dew is not easy to live with; she gets on badly with Michael's mother, she often calls him John instead of Michael, and she ignores his requests to sing her long song, "Precious Lord, take my hand. . . ." His mother wants to get rid of the hundred penny box. "When I lose my hundred penny box, I lose me," says Aunt Dew, and Michael intends to defy his mother and save the box. In the meantime, all he can do is to stay close to Aunt Dew and let her know he loves her. Illustrated by Leo and Diane Dillon, *The Hundred Penny Box* (1975) is a moving book, saluting not only Black children but the old, who have survived and still keep going.

Teacup Full of Roses (1972), an ALA Notable Book, is one of Mathis's two novels for older readers. Joe, who is seventeen, has finished high school at night and is about to graduate. A dreamer and a storyteller, he plans to marry Ellie and take her off to live "in a teacup full of roses." Joe's father, weakened by a heart condition, is unemployed. His mother is blind to all around her except her oldest son, Paul, a talented artist and a drug addict who has already given up on himself. Joe's brother Davey is very bright and a talented athlete. Joe knows that he is the only one on whom Davey can depend. He decides to join the Navy and to leave Davey with enough money to help him make it through college. However, on the night of Joe's graduation, as Aunt Lou had predicted, trouble comes and tragedy occurs. In many ways, *Teacup Full of Roses* is a grim, sad book. But the focus, even in the midst of such sadness, is on Joe's strength, his love for Ellie and for his family, especially Davey, and his "profound sense of survival." He is one who will look back and wonder how he got over, but he *will* get over.

Muffin, the blind sixteen-year-old in *Listen for the Fig Tree*, finds that her blindness is not as difficult to cope with as growing up, especially since her mother turned to alcohol to assuage her grief over the death of Muffin's father last Christmas. In the face of evidence to the contrary, Muffin wants to believe that her mother is improving and that she can therefore concentrate on preparations for Kwanza, an Afro-American celebration that begins Christmas night. Her boyfriend Ernie tells her she is "riding a horse backward." She is helped by Mr. Dale, an upstairs neighbor who taught her to sew and to walk tall; by Reverend Williams, her father's "growin up buddy"; by Miss Geneva, who lives downstairs; and by Mr. Thomas, the old man who comes to her rescue when she is assaulted in the hallway of her building. Muffin almost gives up after the attack, but at the Kwanza ceremony she decides that it is time to "ride the horse forward," to face the reality of her mother's condition and her own growing up, and to find the strength and courage to help them both.

The Mathis image of Afro-American experience adds a dimension that is not found in the work of Clifton, Greenfield, and Hamilton. Her city children must cope with stark conditions and with adults who are capable of cruelty, violence, and other destructive behaviors. Her fiction contrasts with that of Hamilton, who declares: "No one dies in . . . any of my books . . . nor have my fictional Black people become human sacrifices in the name of social accuracy" (1975b, p. 343). Mathis's reality includes some of the hard facts of life with which some contemporary Black children, particularly those growing up in large cities, must cope. Her apparent intention is to suggest that Black children are, and must continue to be, strong enough to survive in spite of those forces and that they have within themselves the resources to do so. In that regard, she is not unlike Hamilton, who continued the above statement in this way: "For young people reading *M.C.*, particularly the poor and the Blacks, have got to realize that his effort with his bare hands to stay alive and save his way of life must be their effort as well. For too long, too many have suffered and died without cause. I prefer to write about those who survive."

For a complete listing of the books by Sharon Bell Mathis discussed in this section, see page 101.

Walter Dean Myers

Walter Dean Myers lives in Jersey City, New Jersey, and is a freelance writer who, in his novels, writes about what he calls "vertical living," living in the city. However, with one exception, his novels, unlike the work of the four previously discussed authors, are marked by a great deal of humor. Zora Neale Hurston (1958), writing about High John, the Conqueror, stated that "Heaven arms with love and laughter those it does not wish to see destroyed" (p. 95). Myers's work focuses on the love and laughter that is part of the Afro-American experience. Besides the novels, he has written some picture books for younger children, including some fantasy and some science fiction. His first published children's book, *Where Does the Day Go?* (1969), focuses on differences—between day and night, between people.

Two of his picture books feature young Black boys. In *The Dancers* (1972), illustrated by Anne Rockwell, Michael meets ballet dancers and invites them "uptown"; the dancers enjoy exchanging dance steps and eating soul food with Michael and his friends. In *Fly, Jimmy, Fly* (1974), Jimmy uses his imagination to set himself flying above the city. It is Myers's unerring ear for Black speech and his inclusion of such details as collard greens and cornbread that make the experiences memorable.

The Dragon Takes a Wife (1972), his third picture book, is a departure—a fairy tale made contemporary, humorous, Afro-American, and controversial. Mabel Mae Jones, one of the sweetest and kindest fairies in the kingdom, tries to help Harry the Dragon win one of his battles with the Knight in Shining Armor so that Harry can win a wife. Mabel Mae is a brown-skinned, Afro-wearing beauty whose first words to Harry are "What's bugging you, baby?" Having decided that "I can dig where you're coming from," she proceeds to try several rhyming incantations, such as "Fire be hotter and hotter than that. Turn Harry on so he can burn that cat." None of them work until she herself turns into a dragon and provides more direct assistance. Some Black teachers and librarians objected to the hip language and to the Geraldine/Flip Wilson-like characterization of Mabel Mae. Some whites, according to Myers (1979), objected to a Black writer's appropriating the West European fairy tale form.

His junior novels won much more acclaim than negative criticism. In a speech at a convention of the National Council of Teachers of English in San Francisco, Myers stated that an author writing about the urban scene must decide "where to put the exclamation points."[1] He felt that there was pressure to emphasize the sensational, the sordid, at the expense of the rest of everyday living in

---

1. W. D. Myers. "Urban Literature." Speech presented at the Convention of the National Council of Teachers of English, November 1979, in San Francisco.

the city, a pressure he resisted. Three of his four novels focus on groups of adolescents growing up, experiencing pain as well as love and laughter, but with the exclamation points behind the love and laughter. All presented in the first person, the novels have the air of adult remembrances of youthful times and youthful friends.

The first novel, *Fast Sam, Cool Clyde, and Stuff* (1975), was an ALA Notable Book. It is narrated by Francis/Stuff and is the story of the 116th Street Good People—the three title characters plus Gloria, Binky, Cap, Maria, and Debbie—who hang out together, support each other, and laugh and cry together. It is episodic, and the group members do deal with pain—Clyde's father is accidentally killed, Gloria's parents split up, Carnation Charlie dies—but mainly they deal with just living, learning, growing—Black urban style.

Mojo and the Russians (1977) features Dean and his gang of friends, including a white girl named Judy. While Kitty and Dean are having a bicycle race, Dean accidentally runs into Druscilla, the West Indian mojo lady, and knocks her down. She, in turn, threatens to "make his tongue split like a lizard's and his eyes to cross" and to "make his monkey ears fall off." Convinced that Druscilla has "fixed" him, Dean and his friends try to get him unfixed. Part of the plan is to find out why the Russians from the Embassy are hanging around with Druscilla's boyfriend, Long Willie. If he is spying, Willie can be whitemailed (you can't black-mail Black people) into making Druscilla lift the spell. Meanwhile, Leslie knows something about mojo and may be able to unfix Dean herself. The situations they get into and out of are hilarious.

In *The Young Landlords* (1979), Paul Williams and his friends from the Action Group—Gloria, Dean Bubba, Omar, and Jeannie—decide that they need to do something constructive with their lives and complain to a landlord about the condition of a tenement on Gloria's block. The landlord decides to abandon the building by selling it to Paul for $1.00. Thus, the group members become the young landlords. In carrying out their responsibilities, they have some fun and discover their own strengths. They also become involved in helping a friend who has been accused of stealing.

The Myers humor, which is never derogatory, stems from a blend of situations, characters, and language. In *Fast Sam, Cool Clyde, and Stuff*, Sam and Clyde (dressed as Claudette) enter and win a dance contest. Another boy makes a pass at Clyde/Claudette, who takes off his wig and punches the offender. In *The Young Landlords*, Askia Ben Kenobi greets the landlords, who have come to collect rent, with "Do not speak until I have grasped the meaning of your aura!" and proceeds to chop up the bannister with karate blows.

But one of Myers's special gifts is his rendering of the style and essence of Black teenage rhetoric. Better than any of the other authors discussed here, he captures many of the rhetorical qualities that Geneva Smitherman describes in *Talkin and Testifyin*—the proverbial statements, such as "Every streak of fat don't have a streak of lean"; the use of tonal semantics, such as "If you got the weight, you got to take the freight"; the image making and the hyperbole, such as "They said he had a gun and would shoot you if you sneezed wrong." He also captures the flavor of the verbal contests that boys (and apparently some girls) engage in. From *Fast Sam, Cool Clyde, and Stuff*: "If you were any uglier, they'd put your face in a museum and sell tickets to gorillas. The worst thing I could say about your mama is that you're her son. . . . If you ask me, you must be the retarded son of the Heartbreak of Psoriasis." And from the sidelines, "Hey Binky, you forgot this is national Be Nice to Ugly Week!" He also illustrates the tendency of Black teenagers to give nicknames that capture some feature of the individual—Weasel, Long Willie, Stuff, Carnation Charlie. Needless to say, he also includes a great number of specific details that bring to life the characters, their environment, and their situations.

The final novel, *It Ain't All for Nothin'* (1978), is not at all humorous. Tippy lives with his religious grandmother until, at sixty-nine, she becomes afflicted badly with arthritis and "old age" and is taken to a nursing home. He must then go to live with his father, Lonnie, an ex-convict who has no concept of how to be a father and who has been making a living by stealing. Lonnie uses Tippy to get on welfare. At one point, Lonnie gets a job and seems about to break out of his pattern, but he is fired after a fight. He decides to pull just one final robbery and coerces Tippy into participating. One of Lonnie's friends, Bubba, is shot in the robbery, and Tippy cannot simply let him die, as Stone, the gang member with the gun, is determined to do. Tippy escapes from the house and seeks the help of a bus driver who had befriended him earlier. They call the police, and Lonnie and the gang are picked up. Even though Bubba dies and Lonnie is returned to prison, Tippy and Lonnie realize that Tippy made the right decision; he *had* to try to save Bubba and thereby save himself.

It Ain't All for Nothin' portrays a different side of city life than in other books by Myers. It is most similar to the Sharon Bell Mathis novels in its inclusion of harsh and grim realities. And, as in the Mathis books, the emphasis seems to be on the boy himself—on his strengths, on his will to save himself, and finally on his hope.

Myers's work, then, mirrors the focus of the other four authors on some of the positive aspects of Afro-American experience—the good times, the idea that the love and the support of family, friends, and community can "prop you up on every leaning side," as a suitor promised in Zora Neale Hurston's *Jonah's Gourd Vine.* It also emphasizes the individual strengths and the inner resources that enable us to cope and to survive.

For a complete listing of the books by Walter Dean Myers discussed in this section, see page 101.

As a group, these five authors—Clifton, Greenfield, Hamilton, Mathis, Myers—have created a significant body of Afro-American children's fiction. Influenced by their own Afro-American experiences and by shared collective memories, they have written books that dance to the rhythms of the same drums. Whether the drums laugh or cry, the work of these authors have common emphases on (1) Afro-American heritage and history; (2) pride in being Black; (3) a sense of community among Blacks; (4) the importance of warm and loving human relationships, particularly within families; (5) a sense of continuity; and, above all, (6) the will and strength and determination to cope and survive.

Absent from their work is any reference to "The Black Problem," any emphasis on desegregation, any emphasis on Black-white conflict. They do not interpret Afro-American experience either in terms of its relationship to white middle-class cultural values or in terms of Black reactions to the oppressive behaviors of non-Blacks. If there is a distinct body of contemporary Afro-American children's fiction, the work of these authors constitutes a significant portion of that literature and goes a long way toward defining its essential characteristics.

Other Afro-American Image-Makers

As has been reported, thirty-four Afro-American authors are represented in this survey. Unfortunately, the purposes of this analysis would not be served by mentioning all thirty-four and reviewing their work, but a few authors should be singled out. Besides the five just discussed, several others have added significantly to the body of Afro-American children's literature in some way.

Although Mildred Taylor has published just two books, one of them was the second book by a Black author to win the coveted

John Newbery Medal. It was also made into a television film, and therefore is widely known. *Roll of Thunder, Hear My Cry* (1976) was set in Mississippi at least a generation ago; it tells of the love and strength of the Logan family and their determination to hold on to the land and their dignity in the face of white oppression. Her first book, *Song of the Trees* (1975), was also about the Logan family, and Taylor has promised a sequel.

Another family that faces and eventually triumphs over white oppression is the Williams family in Lorenz Graham's books, *South Town* (1958), *North Town* (1965), *Whose Town?* (1969), and *Return to South Town* (1976). Graham, the brother-in-law of W.E.B. DuBois, has also produced a series of picture books in which adaptations of Bible stories are told in the English pidgin of Black Liberians early in the century and illustrated in their image by such artists as Ann Grifalconi. They include *Every Man Heart Lay Down* (1970), which is the Christmas story; *A Road Down in the Sea* (1970), the story of Moses leading the Israelites across the Red Sea; *David He No Fear* (1971), the David and Goliath legend; *God Wash the World and Start Again* (1971), the story of the great flood; and *Hongry Catch the Foolish Boy* (1973), the story of the Prodigal Son.

Taylor and Graham, partly because of the time and place in which their novels are set, are almost the only Black authors in the survey to focus on Black-white conflict. But even so, their emphasis is on the Black families, and the conflicts are just some of the obstacles they must overcome to attain their own goals.

Taylor and Graham do fit a pattern common to several Black authors: their books are sequel books in which one character or family becomes the focus of a set of books. Another author who has produced such a set is Rosa Guy, whose books *The Friends* (1973), *Ruby* (1976), and *Edith Jackson* (1978) all revolve around Phylissia, her sister Ruby, and her friend Edith Jackson. Guy's books add another dimension to Afro-American experience, that of the transplanted West Indian living in New York City. In her latest book, *The Disappearance* (1979), Guy moves away from her earlier set of characters, though the West Indian/New York experience is still present. A third author, Brenda Wilkinson, has written three books about a young girl growing up in Waycross, Georgia, and then in New York—*Ludell* (1975), *Ludell and Willie* (1977), and *Ludell's New York Time* (1980). These three authors, like the five discussed at the beginning of the chapter, focus on those aspects of Afro-American experience that they see as positive and important—the determination to survive and the need to lean on each other for love and support.

A discussion of significant image-makers cannot end without mention of at least two major illustrators. Actually, a number of Black artists have illustrated more than one of the books in the survey—Carole Byard, Moneta Barnett, Ray Prather, and the award-winning Leo Dillon, who works with his wife, Diane. But just two illustrators will be briefly discussed here because their work is widely known in the area of realistic fiction.

John Steptoe first came to the attention of the children's book world when he published *Stevie* (1969) while still a teenager. Robert, the narrator, told his story in natural-sounding Black vernacular, unusual in books of that time. It was followed by other picture books that also used Black English (and in the case of the controversial *Uptown* [1970], Black urban slang). His later books became much more personal stories about himself and his two children, such as *My Special Best Words* (1974), which featured the Steptoe children in everyday activities, and his latest, *Daddy Is a Monster . . . Sometimes* (1980). He has also produced one junior novel, *Marcia* (1976), which discusses frankly some of the problems of growing up, such as the decision about when to become sexually active.

Steptoe, however, is primarily an artist, one of the very few Black author/illustrators publishing currently. He has also illustrated books by other authors, including Lucille Clifton and Eloise Greenfield. His art is stylized, sometimes experimental, and, especially in his early work, heavily influenced by African styles and motifs.

The other artist whose work must be mentioned is Tom Feelings, who has illustrated numerous books, including two Caldecott Honor Books, *Moja Means One: Swahili Counting Book* (1971) and *Jambo Means Hello: Swahili Alphabet Book* (1974). Both books were written by his wife, Muriel Feelings. He also illustrated Julius Lester's Newbery Honor Book, *To Be a Slave* (1968). His work is worth mentioning not only because of the awards he has received, but because he is, as John O. Killens (1971) said of him, "a young Black artist whose art is a monument to Black life in America. He renders a toast to life in every stroke of his talented brush" (p. 387).

In his own book, *Black Pilgrimage* (1972), Feelings shares some of his art, some of his experiences, and some of his thinking. He has been illustrating children's books since the late sixties and has, through his art, been committed to helping Black children to know and appreciate their own beauty, to see themselves as essentially African peoples, and to recognize that the strength that enables them to survive is not an individual force, but a collective one. His work is beautiful, his contribution extraordinary.

Conclusion

The questions that this chapter attempts to answer are (1) Who are the important image-makers who create from an Afro-American perspective? and (2) What distinguishes their work from those works created from different perspectives? The first question was answered directly. The second question was answered in terms of the themes and emphases that recur in their books. In another sense, however, the answer to the second question is simultaneously more simple and complex than that—what distinguishes the work of these image-makers is the perspective from which they view Afro-American experience. Their perspective makes it necessary for them as writers and artists to be witnesses to Afro-American experience; for Afro-American children to find themselves and their experiences mirrored in this fiction; for Afro-American children to understand "how we got over" in the past and to recognize and develop the inner strengths that will enable them to "get over" in their own times.

Books by the Image-Makers

Lucille Clifton

The Black BC's. Illus. by Don Miller. New York: E. P. Dutton, 1970.

Some of the Days of Everett Anderson. Illus. by Evaline Ness. New York: Holt, Rinehart and Winston, 1970.

Everett Anderson's Christmas Coming. Illus. by Evaline Ness. New York: Holt, Rinehart and Winston, 1971.

All Us Come Cross the Water. Illus. by John Steptoe. New York: Holt, Rinehart and Winston, 1973.

The Boy Who Didn't Believe in Spring. Illus. by Brinton Turkle. New York: E. P. Dutton, 1973.

Don't You Remember? Illus. by Evaline Ness. New York: E. P. Dutton, 1973.

Good, Says Jerome. Illus. by Stephanie Douglas. New York: E. P. Dutton, 1973.

Everett Anderson's Year. Illus. by Ann Grifalconi. New York: Holt, Rinehart and Winston, 1974.

The Times They Used to Be. Illus. by Susan Jeschke. New York: Holt, Rinehart and Winston, 1974.

My Brother Fine with Me. Illus. by Moneta Barnett. New York: Holt, Rinehart and Winston, 1975.

Everett Anderson's Friend. Illus. by Ann Grifalconi. New York: Holt, Rinehart and Winston, 1976.

Everett Anderson's 1-2-3. Illus. by Ann Grifalconi. New York: Holt, Rinehart and Winston, 1976.

The Three Wishes. Illus. by Stephanie Douglas. New York: Viking Press, 1976.

Amifika. Illus. by Thomas DiGrazia. New York: E. P. Dutton, 1977.

Everett Anderson's Nine Month Long. Illus. by Ann Grifalconi. New York: Holt, Rinehart and Winston, 1978.

The Lucky Stone. Illus. by Dale Payson. New York: Delacorte Press, 1979.

My Friend Jacob. Illus. by Thomas DiGrazia. New York: E. P. Dutton, 1980.

Eloise Greenfield

Good News. Illus. by Pat Cummings. New York: Coward, McCann and Geoghegan, 1977. Originally published as *Bubbles,* 1972.

Rosa Parks. Illus. by Eric Marlow. New York: Thomas Y. Crowell, 1973.

She Come Bringing Me That Little Baby Girl. Illus. by John Steptoe. Philadelphia: J. B. Lippincott, 1974.

Sister. Illus. by Moneta Barnett. New York: Thomas Y. Crowell, 1974.

Me and Nessie. Illus. by Moneta Barnett. New York: Thomas Y. Crowell, 1975.

Paul Robeson. Illus. by George Ford. New York: Thomas Y. Crowell, 1975.

First Pink Light. Illus. by Moneta Barnett. New York: Thomas Y. Crowell, 1976.

Africa Dream. Illus. by Carole Byard. New York: John Day Co., 1977.

Mary McLeod Bethune. Illus. by Jerry Pinkney. New York: Thomas Y. Crowell, 1977.

Honey, I Love and Other Poems. Illus. by Leo and Diane Dillon. New York: Thomas Y. Crowell, 1978.

I Can Do It by Myself. Illus. by Carole Byard. New York: Thomas Y. Crowell, 1978. (Co-authored with Lessie Jones Little)

Talk about a Family. Illus. by James Calvin. Philadelphia: J. B. Lippincott, 1978.

Childtimes: A Three Generation Memoir. Illus. by Jerry Pinkney. New York: Thomas Y. Crowell, 1979. (Co-authored with Lessie Jones Little)

Virginia Hamilton

Zeely. New York: Macmillan, 1967.

The Time-Ago Tales of Jahdu. New York: Macmillan, 1969.

The House of Dies Drear. New York: Macmillan, 1970.

The Planet of Junior Brown. New York: Macmillan, 1972.

W.E.B. DuBois: A Biography. New York: Thomas Y. Crowell, 1972.

Time-Ago Lost: More Tales of Jahdu. New York: Thomas Y. Crowell, 1973.

M.C. Higgins, the Great. New York: Macmillan, 1974.

Paul Robeson: The Life and Times of a Free Black Man. New York: Harper and Row, 1974.

The Writings of W.E.B. DuBois. New York: Thomas Y. Crowell, 1975. (Edited by Virginia Hamilton)

Arilla Sun Down. New York: Greenwillow Books, 1976.

Justice and Her Brothers. New York: Greenwillow Books, 1978.

Dustland. New York: Greenwillow Books, 1980.
The Gathering. New York: Greenwillow Books, 1980.

Sharon Bell Mathis

Brooklyn Story. New York: Hill and Wang, 1970.
Sidewalk Story. Illus. by Leo Carty. New York: Viking Press, 1971.
Teacup Full of Roses. New York: Viking Press, 1972.
Ray Charles. Illus. by George Ford. New York: Thomas Y. Crowell, 1973.
Listen for the Fig Tree. New York: Viking Press, 1974.
The Hundred Penny Box. Illus. by Leo and Diane Dillon. New York: Viking Press, 1975.

Walter Dean Myers

Where Does the Day Go? New York: Parents Magazine Press, 1969.
The Dancers. Illus. by Anne Rockwell. New York: Parents Magazine Press, 1972.
The Dragon Takes a Wife. Illus. by Ann Grifalconi. Indianapolis: Bobbs-Merrill, 1972.
Fly, Jimmy, Fly. Illus. by Moneta Barnett. New York: G. P. Putnam's Sons, 1974.
Fast Sam, Cool Clyde, and Stuff. New York: Viking Press, 1975.
Mojo and the Russians. New York: Viking Press, 1977.
It Ain't All for Nothin'. New York: Viking Press, 1978.
The Young Landlords. New York: Viking Press, 1979.

Other Afro-American Image-Makers

Feelings, Muriel. *Moja Means One: Swahili Counting Book.* Illus. by Tom Feelings. New York: Dial Press, 1971.
Feelings, Muriel. *Jambo Means Hello: Swahili Alphabet Book.* New York: Dial Press, 1974.
Feelings, Tom. *Black Pilgrimage.* New York: Lothrop, Lee and Shepard, 1972.
Graham, Lorenz. *South Town.* Chicago: Follett, 1958.
Graham, Lorenz. *North Town.* New York: Thomas Y. Crowell, 1965.
Graham, Lorenz. *Whose Town?* New York: Thomas Y. Crowell, 1969.
Graham, Lorenz. *Every Man Heart Lay Down.* Illus. by Colleen Browning. New York: Thomas Y. Crowell, 1970.
Graham, Lorenz. *A Road Down in the Sea.* Illus. by Gregorio Prestopino. New York: Thomas Y. Crowell, 1970.
Graham, Lorenz. *David He No Fear.* Illus. by Ann Grifalconi. New York: Thomas Y. Crowell, 1971.
Graham, Lorenz. *God Wash the World and Start Again.* Illus. by Clare Ross. New York: Thomas Y. Crowell, 1971.
Graham, Lorenz. *Hongry Catch the Foolish Boy.* Illus. by James Brown, Jr. New York: Thomas Y. Crowell, 1973.

Graham, Lorenz. *Return to South Town.* New York: Thomas Y. Crowell, 1976.

Guy, Rosa. *The Friends.* New York: Holt, Rinehart and Winston, 1973.

Guy, Rosa. *Ruby.* New York: Viking Press, 1976.

Guy, Rosa. *Edith Jackson.* New York: Viking Press, 1978.

Guy, Rosa. *The Disappearance.* New York: Delacorte Press, 1979.

Lester, Julius. *To Be a Slave.* Illus. by Tom Feelings. New York: Dial Press, 1968.

Steptoe, John. *Stevie.* New York: Harper and Row, 1969.

Steptoe, John. *Uptown.* New York: Harper and Row, 1970.

Steptoe, John. *Birthday.* New York: Holt, Rinehart and Winston, 1972.

Steptoe, John. *My Special Best Words.* New York: Viking Press, 1974.

Steptoe, John. *Marcia.* New York: Viking Press, 1976.

Steptoe, John. *Daddy Is a Monster . . . Sometimes.* Philadelphia: J. B. Lippincott, 1980.

Taylor, Mildred. *Song of the Trees.* Illus. by Jerry Pinkney. New York: Dial Press, 1975.

Taylor, Mildred. *Roll of Thunder, Hear My Cry.* New York: Dial Press, 1976.

Wilkinson, Brenda. *Ludell.* New York: Harper and Row, 1975.

Wilkinson, Brenda. *Ludell and Willie.* New York: Harper and Row, 1977.

Wilkinson, Brenda. *Ludell's New York Time.* New York: Harper and Row, 1980.

6 Where Are We?
Where Do We Go from Here?

We may not be where we want to be,
We may not be where we're going to be,
But thank God Almighty
We ain't where we was!

Anonymous Afro-American Preacher

This survey and analysis of contemporary realistic fiction about Afro-Americans has sought to evaluate the response of the children's book world to the challenge of the 1960s, particularly the widely publicized charge by Nancy Larrick (1965) that the world of children's books was all-white. Since Chall et al. (1979) had already declared that by 1975 the quantitative response had been substantial, this analysis has attempted to meet the need for an in-depth examination of the content and quality of books about Afro-Americans.

Where Are We?

Fiction about Afro-Americans seems to have had one of three major socializing purposes: to promote racial harmony, to promote American cultural homogeneity, or to provide self-affirmation for Afro-American children. During the period of the survey, 1965–1979, the trend has been toward a decrease of books promoting racial harmony and an increase in books reflecting the distinctiveness of the Afro-American experience. Books promoting cultural homogeneity are sprinkled throughout the period. This may indicate a trend away from the inclusion of Black children merely as subjects in literature to a consideration of Afro-American children as audience as well.

In view of Broderick's (1973) assertion that the books she examined up to 1967 represented "what the white establishment wanted white children to know about Blacks" (p. 6), it seems reasonable to ask whether, in the past fifteen years, some consid-

103

eration has been given to what Afro-Americans want both white and Black children to know. The reviews are mixed, so to speak.

The 150 books in this survey were produced by 104 different authors, only 34 of whom are Black. Looked at another way, 80 of the 150 books (53 percent) were produced by non-Blacks. Not surprisingly, almost all of the 34 Black authors produced books of the culturally conscious/self-affirming type. Since the trend is toward an increase in that type of book, it might appear that there is cause for rejoicing. However, it should also be pointed out that 28 percent of the culturally conscious books were produced by non-Blacks. Thus, to the extent that this survey is representative, it can be said that a substantial portion of the fiction about Afro-Americans is still being filtered through the consciousness, sensibilities, and often ethnocentric world views of non-Afro-American authors.

One of the major purposes of this study has been to ferret out and to demonstrate by example the impact that such a perspective has on the content of fiction about Afro-Americans. In general, the books written to promote racial harmony—the social conscience books, none of which were written by Blacks—are flawed. They are overwhelmed by their social purpose, and too often view their Afro-American subjects from some lofty height, as the instruments for the moral salvation of their protagonists. The melting pot books are a step forward. They eliminate many of the negative aspects of other books. However, as a general group, they also tend to see the world with color-blind vision, or with blinders that permit only part of the world to be seen at a time. Almost all of the melting pot books were written by non-Blacks, but the 12.5 percent that were not reflect the fact that Afro-Americans are simultaneously a part of general American culture and members of a distinct cultural group. The effect of cultural perspective on the culturally conscious books is seen in those aspects of Afro-American living that an author chooses to emphasize and in the richness and accuracy of the specific details an author includes. Unfortunately, in a few cases a few white authors have the arrogance to continue to re-create Amos and Andy, who, after all, originally were white men grasping at the shadows of Black life and humor.

The most optimistic news is that in the past fifteen years a body of Afro-American children's fiction has developed that clearly reflects Afro-American cultural traditions, sensibilities, and world view. It presents an image of Afro-Americans as courageous survivors with a strong sense of community and cultural affinity and with positive feelings about being Black. It presents Afro-American children as strong, resilient, capable, and confident. Like much of the "new realism" of which it is a part, it includes the negative experiences that some Afro-Americans must endure. Its focus is on the human relationships and inner resources that provide support and comfort and strength. This is a far cry from some of the images in the social conscience books, and even farther from the images Broderick found in her historical study. To date, this fiction has been produced by a relatively small group of authors. (Six authors account for 33 percent of the 70 books by Blacks in the total survey. Another four or five would account for almost all Black authors who have published more than two books of fiction for children.) More such authors need to be found and encouraged.

In that regard, the work of at least one organization should be mentioned because of its efforts to improve the image of minorities and increase the numbers of minority authors in the world of children's books. When Larrick was writing her article, the Council on Interracial Books for Children was a fledgling organization. Since then, it has been responsible for increasing the representation of minorities in children's books and for increasing awareness of racism, sexism, and other antihuman values in children's books. A number of its annual contest winners have gone on to be published, and some have won major awards: *Sidewalk Story* by Sharon Bell Mathis, *The Soul Brothers and Sister Lou* by Kristin Hunter, *Song of the Trees* by Mildred Taylor, and *Ashanti to Zulu: African Traditions* by Margaret Musgrove (New York: Dial Press, 1976).

From this council (Chambers;[1] Myers, 1979) comes confirmation of an impression that quantitatively the current news is not as good as it had been in the past. There is a saying among Afro-Americans, "What goes 'round, comes 'round," and it seems that what has come around is another lean period in the publishing of books about Afro-Americans. Myers declared that fewer such books are currently being published than a decade ago. Chambers reported that there has been a substantial decrease in the last few years in the numbers of books about Blacks being sent to the council for review. The claims of the council are supported by a recent survey (Walter and Volc, 1980). A questionnaire was sent to fifty major publishers, twenty-six of whom replied. Of those, sixteen publishers indicated they had published books about

---

1. B. Chambers. Personal communication, May 1980.

Blacks between 1975 and 1979. Of a total of 1,780 books brought out by those publishers in those years, only 24 (1.3 percent) were written by Black writers, only 7 books in 1979. Further, ten respondents indicated that they felt the market for Black writers had decreased in recent years.

It is not clear whether this trend reflects the economy in general, an upsurge in conservatism, a "backlash" effect, or just a general lack of commitment on the part of publishers to make and keep the world of children's literature a pluralistic one. In any case, it is a disturbing trend.

Where Do We Go from Here?

The record suggests that not enough Afro-American literature is being published. The Walter and Volc study also surveyed librarians, who indicated a willingness to spend up to one-fourth of their budgets on books by and about Blacks, if such books were available. According to the Chall study, approximately 86 percent of the world of children's books was still all-white in 1975. Clearly, more Afro-American authors of children's fiction need to be supported and permitted to develop their talents. There is a wealth of Afro-American experience yet to be mined.

There are still more contemporary realistic stories to be told, set in different places, focusing on different themes. There is also much to be done in other genre as well. With a few notable exceptions, such as Julius Lester's *Black Folk Tales* (1969), there is very little published in the way of Afro-American (as distinct from African) folklore for children, and there is much folklore available to be tapped. Additionally, the history of Afro-Americans, which neither began nor ended with slavery, is rich with stories yet to be told, both factually and in the form of historical fiction. Chall et al. also reported that while there were many biographies of Blacks available, the vast majority were of athletes and entertainers. While there is some poetry, there is room for much more. One area that is almost totally neglected in terms of Afro-Americans as major characters is modern fantasy. And there is an abundance of nonfiction yet to be written—recipe books, craft books (such as a book on quilting patterns), books about the Black church, and numerous other topics.

Finally, there needs to be a major effort to reach the potential market for Afro-American literature. It is unrealistic to expect publishers to produce books that they believe will not sell. At the same time, it would profit them to find innovative ways to reach the substantial Black-American economic market that exists (the Reverend Jesse Jackson [*Ebony*, 1981] speaks of a $125 billion Black consumer base) and to do a better job of promoting books about Afro-Americans in their dealings with bookstores. There is an appalling lack of information among the general public about the availability of such books, and even those who know about their existence must usually place special orders for them with bookstores. A Black parent has a difficult time finding good quality Afro-American literature, even when it has been published. Ads in the *New York Times Book Review, The Horn Book Magazine,* and trade journals apparently do not reach the Black buying public.

In light of all the recent publicity about the so-called decline in literacy among Americans and the continuing publicity to the effect that Black American children as a group fare worse in reading than white American children as a group, there is a strong argument for increasing the availability of reading material in which Afro-Americans see themselves. There is some evidence that readers who are members of nonwhite groups in this country can perform better when reading stories that reflect the world as they know it than when reading stories that do not. For example, Goodman and Goodman (1978), in a study of the oral reading of children from eight American language groups including some Mississippi Blacks, had all children read one story that was standard across groups (within grade levels) and one that was "culturally relevant." They found higher retelling scores for culturally relevant stories than for the standard ones.

Publishers, however, cannot be held solely responsible. The market for Afro-American literature will be relatively small unless teachers and librarians, as well as publishers, recognize that Afro-American children's literature should no more be restricted to Black children than Isaac Bashevis Singer's books should be restricted to Jewish children. Afro-American literature is *necessary* for Black children, but it is also essential for non-Black children. As Larrick argued fifteen years ago:

> The impact of all-white books on 39,600,000 white children is probably even worse. Although his light skin makes him one of the world's minorities, the white child learns from his books that he is the kingfish. There seems little chance of developing the humility needed for world cooperation instead of world conflict, as long as our children are brought up on gentle doses of racism through their books. [P. 63]

In the political environment of the early eighties, the argument that the kingfish child needs to develop humility may not set well, but the idea that white American children need to know that they are part, and a minority part at that, of a multicultural, pluralistic world is still valid and will continue to be. The political climate in the United States has changed considerably since 1965. The Civil Rights Movement seems strangely quiet. White males, threatened with the loss of privilege by the rise of minorities and women, have carried their charge of "reverse discrimination" to the Supreme Court. The Ku Klux Klan, with its Harvard-educated leader, is on one of its periodic upswings. A quarter of a century after *Brown v. Topeka*, a federal judge and a state judge in Louisiana engaged in a battle over school desegregation, and Chicago was still fighting over its school desegregation plan. What goes 'round, comes 'round. One has to wonder if and how this will all be reflected in the field of children's literature.

This survey has indicated that the children's book world has not yet regressed to its former pale condition. There has been progress in the efforts to desegregate the world of children's books. We are *not* where we want to be, since gentle doses of racism are still being offered through children's books. But with cautious optimism we can report that we are also *not* where we were.

References

Alexander, R. "What Is a Racist Book?" *Interracial Books for Children Bulletin* 3 (1970): 1, 5, 7.

Baker, H. *The Journey Back: Issues in Black Literature and Criticism.* Chicago: University of Chicago Press, 1980.

Blauner, R. "Black Culture: Myth or Reality?" In *Afro-American Anthropology*, edited by N. Whitten and J. F. Szwed. New York: Free Press, 1970.

Broderick, D. *Image of the Black in Children's Fiction.* New York: R. R. Bowker, 1973.

Chall, J.; Radwin, E.; French, V.; and Hall, C. "Blacks in the World of Children's Books." *The Reading Teacher* 32 (1979): 527-33.

Clifton, L. *Generations: A Memoir.* New York: Random House, 1976.

Ebony interview with the Reverend Jesse Jackson. *Ebony*, June 1981, pp. 155-62.

Gerald, C. "The Black Writer and His Role." In *The Black Aesthetic*, edited by A. Gayle. Garden City, N. Y.: Doubleday, 1972.

Goodman, K. S., and Goodman, Y. M. *Reading of American Children Whose Language Is a Stable Rural Dialect of English or a Language Other Than English.* Final Report, Project NIE-C-00-3-0087. Washington, D.C.: U.S. Department of Health, Education and Welfare, National Institute of Education, August 1978.

Greenfield, E. "Something to Shout About." *The Horn Book Magazine* 51 (December 1975): 624-26.

Hamilton, V. *Paul Robeson: The Life and Times of a Free Black Man.* New York: Harper and Row, 1974.

Hamilton, V. "High John Is Risen Again." *The Horn Book Magazine* 51 (April 1975a): 113-21.

Hamilton, V. "Newbery Award Acceptance." *The Horn Book Magazine* 51 (August 1975b): 337-43.

Hamilton, V. "Writing the Source: In Other Words." *The Horn Book Magazine* 54 (December 1978): 609-19.

Heins, E. L. Review of *Philip Hall Likes Me, I Reckon, Maybe*, by B. Greene. *The Horn Book Magazine* 51 (April 1975): 149.

Huck, C. *Children's Literature in the Elementary School.* 3d ed. New York: Holt, Rinehart and Winston, 1979.

Hurston, Z. N. "High John de Conquer." In *The Book of Negro Folklore*, edited by L. Hughes and A. Bontemps. New York: Dodd, Mead and Co., 1958.

Kiah, R. "Profile: Eloise Greenfield." *Language Arts* 57 (1980): 653–59.

Killens, J. O. "The Black Writer vis-à-vis His Country." In *The Black Aesthetic*, edited by A. Gayle. Garden City, N. Y.: Doubleday, 1972.

Larrick, N. "The All-White World of Children's Books." *Saturday Review* 11 (September 1965): 63–65, 84–85.

Latimer, B. I., ed. *Starting Out Right: Choosing Books about Blacks for Young People.* Madison, Wis.: Department of Public Instruction, 1972.

Levine, L. *Black Culture and Black Consciousness: Afro-American Folk Thought from Slavery to Freedom.* New York: Oxford University Press, 1977.

McCann, D., and Woodard, G., eds. *The Black American in Books for Children: Readings in Racism.* Metuchen, N.J.: Scarecrow Press, 1972.

Myers, W. "The Black Experience in Children's Books: One Step Forward, Two Steps Back." *Interracial Books for Children Bulletin* 10 (1979): 14–15.

Rollock, B., ed. *The Black Experience in Children's Books.* New York: New York Public Library, 1974 and 1979.

Rudman, M. K. *Children's Literature: An Issues Approach.* Boston: D. C. Heath, 1976.

Shepard, R. A. "Adventures in Blackland with Keats and Steptoe." *Interracial Books for Children Bulletin* 3 (1971): 2–3.

Smitherman, G. *Talkin and Testifyin: The Language of Black America.* Boston: Houghton Mifflin, 1977.

Walter, M. P., and Volc, J. "What's Ahead for the Black Writer?" *Publishers Weekly*, 25 July 1980: 90–92.

Watkins, M. "James Baldwin Writing and Talking." *New York Times Book Review* 23 (September 1979): 3, 36–37.

Woods, G., and Lester, J. "Black and White: An Exchange." In *The Black American in Books for Children: Readings in Racism*, edited by D. McCann and G. Woodard. Metuchen, N. J.: Scarecrow Press, 1972.

Wright, R. "Introduction: Blueprint for Negro Writing." In *The Black Aesthetic*, edited by A. Gayle. Garden City, N. Y.: Doubleday, 1972.

Author

Rudine Sims received degrees in Elementary Education and Curriculum Development from West Chester State College, Pennsylvania, the University of Pennsylvania, and Wayne State University, Michigan. After having taught at both the elementary and college level, she is currently Professor of Education at the University of Massachusetts, Amherst. She has published numerous articles and reviews in a variety of scholarly journals.